MW00572081

# FIGHTING SHADOWS

# FIGHTING SHADOWS

JEFFERSON
**BETHKE**
AND
JON
**TYSON**

NELSON
BOOKS
An Imprint of Thomas Nelson

Published in Nashville, Tennessee, by Nelson Books, an imprint of Thomas Nelson. Nelson Books and Thomas Nelson are registered trademarks of HarperCollins Christian Publishing, Inc.

Published in association with Yates & Yates, www.yates2.com.

Thomas Nelson titles may be purchased in bulk for educational, business, fundraising, or sales promotional use. For information, please email SpecialMarkets@ThomasNelson.com.

Unless otherwise noted, Scripture quotations are taken from The Holy Bible, New International Version®, NIV®. Copyright © 1973, 1978, 1984, 2011 by Biblica, Inc.® Used by permission of Zondervan. All rights reserved worldwide. www.Zondervan.com. The "NIV" and "New International Version" are trademarks registered in the United States Patent and Trademark Office by Biblica, Inc.®

Scripture quotations marked KJV are taken from the King James Version. Public domain.

Scripture quotations marked NASB are taken from the New American Standard Bible® (NASB). Copyright © 1960, 1962, 1963, 1968, 1971, 1972, 1973, 1975, 1977, 1995 by The Lockman Foundation. Used by permission. www.lockman.org

Scripture quotations marked NKJV are taken from the New King James Version®. Copyright © 1982 by Thomas Nelson. Used by permission. All rights reserved.

Scripture quotations marked NLT are taken from the Holy Bible, New Living Translation. © 1996, 2004, 2015 by Tyndale House Foundation. Used by permission of Tyndale House Publishers, Inc., Carol Stream, Illinois 60188. All rights reserved.

Scripture quotations marked PHILLIPS are taken from The New Testament in Modern English by J. B. Phillips. Copyright © 1960, 1972 J. B. Phillips. Administered by the Archbishops' Council of the Church of England. Used by permission.

Any internet addresses, phone numbers, or company or product information printed in this book are offered as a resource and are not intended in any way to be or to imply an endorsement by Thomas Nelson, nor does Thomas Nelson vouch for the existence, content, or services of these sites, phone numbers, companies, or products beyond the life of this book.

ISBN 978-1-4002-4332-7 (audiobook)
ISBN 978-1-4002-4331-0 (ePub)
ISBN 978-1-4002-4824-7 (ITPE)
ISBN 978-1-4002-4330-3 (HC)

**Library of Congress Control Number: 2023952520**

*Printed in the United States of America*
24 25 26 27 28 LBC 5 4 3 2 1

# CONTENTS

# INTRODUCTION

The Lie of the Shadows

They can only come to morning through the shadows.

—J. R. R. TOLKIEN

You don't find light by avoiding the darkness.

—S. KELLEY HARRELL

**It was September 2021, in Woodstock, Vermont,**
(rated Top 10 idyllic small town Main streets for fall in the
nation). The leaves were "peak," as they say in the Northeast,
and we were wearing flannels—at least I was (Jeff)—and we were
sitting by a fire inside a cabin on a five-hundred-acre farm.

While at first glance it sounds like a Hallmark movie and
most suited for time with Alyssa, my wife, it was Jon and I,
hosting a retreat for thirty or so pastors. During "The Art of
Teaching" retreat, we tried to unpack our best stuff on communication, preaching, technique, and so on. It was one of the first
events we had hosted together.

The retreat had just ended, and we were debriefing in the living room late at night. And like all good things we are passionate

about, the discussion quickly went from debriefing the retreat to other deep things on our hearts.

That's when we began chatting about how much our hearts ache for men in this current cultural moment. So many of our friends, as well as many of the men in Jon's church, expressed experiencing confusion, shame, and fear on a daily basis. Every time Jon talked about what he saw in his work as a pastor, I yelled, "Me too! I see that too."

And anytime I shared, he responded the same. (It was akin to the famous Spider-Man meme in which two Spider-Mans are pointing at each other—if you don't know it, well, then, never mind.)

We realized we felt that talking to men and about men hit on both our core callings, which were dormant and hadn't been quite yet fully activated. Since that initial discussion, we've given it all we have and started a ministry, launched a nonprofit, and hosted conferences and retreats all over the nation—basically we've tried to serve men in every way you can think of. We've even doubled down since the beginning because the energy given back to us was overwhelming in the best way possible. Guys needed it!

But the very, very, very first project we said we should do? In that conversation around the fire in Vermont?

*This book.*

I said, "Jon, there's so much here. We need to write a book on this. There are not many books for men that are for this moment in time and answer the questions men are asking right now."

Three years later, that is what you're reading right now. It's been a joy to work on and we've given it everything we've got, so we hope you enjoy!

. . .

By 336 BC, Alexander the Great had conquered most of the known world. His empire stretched from Greece to Persia and everywhere between. He had exported Greek culture—the norms, values, art, and customs of his kingdom—across his empire. He had founded more than twenty cities that had become centers of culture, diversity, and power.

Alexander was a brilliant thinker and leader, already well on his way to establishing an unparalleled legacy. His army was legendary for its boldness and skill, and Alexander himself was known as a man of remarkable courage. He was the most powerful man in the world at this time. Alexander was not a man you could take lightly, not a man you could defy and live to tell about it.

Alexander was on a world victory tour of sorts when he came to the city of Corinth. The city came out to see him and congratulate him on all he had accomplished. The great philosophers came to the celebrations, and the city leaders were jubilant. But one notable man was missing from the crowd, the one man Alexander had hoped would come to celebrate him:

Diogenes of Sinope.

Diogenes was somewhat of a wild man.

A controversial figure shrouded in myth, he was one of the founders of the philosophical system of cynicism that morphed into the philosophy of stoicism. He eventually settled in the city of Corinth, where he developed quite a reputation for his counter-cultural lifestyle, denunciations of the powerful and hypocritical, and harsh (often hilarious) critiques of Plato. Before that, he'd been captured by pirates, sold into slavery, and had plenty of other adventures one would hardly expect of a philosopher.

Alexander had to meet a man like that.

But Diogenes had skipped the victory parade of the most powerful man in the world and was sunbathing in the Corinthian suburb of Craneion.

Alexander, in disbelief, went to see Diogenes in person.

When Alexander arrived, there was Diogenes, lying in the sun. Diogenes raised himself up to see the great crowd of statesmen and leaders accompanying Alexander for the meeting. Alexander came and stood over Diogenes, and still Diogenes refused to stand in the presence of the most powerful man in the world. He simply locked eyes with him and said nothing. Alexander greeted him and then asked if there was anything he could do for Diogenes.

"Yes," Diogenes said. "You can get out of my light."

At which point he closed his eyes and continued to sunbathe.

Alexander was stunned. *What sort of man is this?* He walked away and exclaimed, "But truly, if I were not Alexander, I would then wish I were Diogenes!"

Just imagine. The most powerful man in the world stands over you, asking if he can do anything for you.

*Yes. You can get out of my light.*

*You are blocking it with your shadow and it's annoying.*

Where do you get courage like this?

Where do you get the confidence?

And where do you get men who think like this today?

# THE SHADOWS HOVERING OVER US

A low-grade angst seems to have settled over the hearts of men in our world today. You probably know exactly what I'm talking about.

This angst is not new. Writing in the mid-1840s, Henry David Thoreau identified it this way: "The mass of men lead lives of quiet desperation . . . unconscious despair is concealed even under what are called the games and amusements of mankind."[1]

This unconscious despair is not so much a direct threat as a kind of fog that has rolled in, blocking our vision and leaving us confused about how to function as men in the modern world. In some ways the world is still built by men, for men. But in other ways, masculinity itself seems to be in crisis.

There are the obvious attacks on God's creational distinctions for men and women. People today, for example, are asking whether there is even such a thing as *man* (or *woman*) that anyone in our world can agree on. But that's not the main thing confronting most of our hearts. For followers of Jesus, it's about how our vision of being godly men has fallen so far short of our calling. We just don't know how to live from full hearts and hold our heads high as men in the modern world.

> For followers of Jesus, it's about how our vision of being godly men has fallen so far short of our calling.

We feel this angst deeply. We get worried that we are going to say the wrong thing about the latest progressive gender ideas and get lambasted by friends. We are torn about our ambition and how to use it in a way that doesn't hurt others. We are tempted and confused by the sexualization of our world and often feel paralyzed by shame. We feel isolated and don't know how to express our loneliness and vulnerability.

Yet we go to church each week, handle our responsibilities the best we can, and keep gutting it out. The angst lies below the surface, and we are not sure how to get it out.

If we bring this up at church, especially if we are in positions of leadership, we are not sure how our questions will be received because the church today is reeling from the damage men have done.

Our models and mentors have failed us.

Some of our most charismatic pastors seem to be narcissists, some of our most famous apologists have turned out to be predators, and too often the leaders calling for men to lay down their lives like Christ are the ones covering up abuse. Theological discussions about gender roles in the church have boiled over into increasingly divisive social media wars.

It seems the idea of being a Christian man in the world today has largely failed.

And most of us don't just feel this failure in the church—we feel it in our hearts. It's not just that our models have failed us; we deal with the shame of our own failures. So many temptations overwhelm us daily that it can feel like we are waging a war on a thousand fronts.

- How do we work with diligence when we are underemployed?

- How do we stay present with our kids when the world takes the best we have and leaves us scraps for those we love?
- How do we remain involved and invested in our marriages when spouses today are being pulled away from each other by a never-ending list of competing priorities?
- How do we remain faithful in our singleness when faithfulness is viewed with deep suspicion?
- How do we channel our ambition in a redemptive direction without leaving casualties behind us?
- How do we cultivate our dreams in a state of feeling overwhelmed?

And then there are the cultural issues. Many today talk about the need to get rid of toxic masculinity, but it seems what they are really trying to get rid of is masculinity itself. We live in a world where people can't talk about men and masculinity without rolling their eyes, and yet gender-fluid people are held up as heroes of authenticity. We live in a world that tells us being a man is just a social construct and anyone who believes otherwise is an oppressive bigot. We live in a world where masculine strength is dismissed as patriarchy. Men today are supposed to be calm, placid, agreeable, nice, apologetic, and remorseful. We are supposed to sit back, shut up, and hand things over because we have already had our turn.

> We live in a world where you are told being a man is just a social construct and anyone who believes otherwise is an oppressive bigot.

# THREE PROBLEMATIC REACTIONS
# TO THE SHADOWS

When we men see the failures of the church and hear the cultural critiques, it's hard not to simply react. But reacting too quickly can lead to serious missteps. In our years of working in men's ministries, we've generally seen men take three missteps in their reactions to the shadows falling over their hearts.

- *Overcompensate*. Faced with criticism, we may be tempted to double down on traditional gender roles with aggression and defiance. *Men are not just to lead but to dominate, crush, fight, and control*—even if we may not say it in so many words, that attitude can all too easily slip into our thinking and behavior. The cultural stereotypes are obvious here, but when this spirit is dragged into the church, we end up as cartoon men, defined by the flesh. This doesn't look like Jesus, who showed the full range of human emotions, including empathy and tears.

- *Shut down*. Alternately, we may believe the best way to protect our necks is by not sticking them out in the first place. So we bottle our passion and replace it with passivity. We keep our thoughts to ourselves and nod our heads even when we disagree with what's going on around us because we don't have the energy for another pointless fight. We learn to say and do the "right" things. We try to just get through life without ruffling anyone's feathers.

- *Medicate*. Finally, it is incredibly tempting to grab hold of anything that distracts from frustrations or mutes the pain of disappointment. Escapism comes in a multitude of forms. For some it is porn, the fantasy world where compliant women exist to please. For others it is hobbies, video games, and watching sports that give the sense of accomplishment or battle without exertion or risk. For others it is food—driving to the mall for another favorite meal or getting something dropped off by Uber Eats. Or maybe it is as simple as losing ourselves in another Netflix show. We become passive consumers of comforting or entertaining illusions that help us escape the hostility outside.

What these reactionary missteps all have in common is they deaden our hearts and deform us further into the very thing we hate: reactive men who don't know how to find their place and live up to their role in God's story. Slowly we just shrink back. We float. We let our visions fade, strengths atrophy, hearts die. We drift from the light into the shadows.

## SHADOW MEN

The writer of Ecclesiastes said, "For who knows what is good for a man during his lifetime, during the few years of his futile life? He will spend them *like a shadow*" (6:12 NASB, emphasis added).

Spending our lives like shadows, confused about what's good for a man—this has become the fate of so many men. It might even feel like your fate right now.

Several years ago, I (Jon) had a haunting encounter with a man I looked up to when I was a young leader. This man was a public figure who seemed to live an exemplary life. Articulate, strong, charismatic, he was what we all aspired to be like in those years. But he fell, and badly. He gradually drifted out of the limelight and disappeared, forgotten by the evangelical culture as so many leaders are. Years later when I ran into him, my heart broke. Here was a man with gifts that had once stirred hearts and inspired people to action. But now I was looking at a man who got lost along the way, a man in whom the glimmer of life was gone. I will never forget the words my wife said with a broken heart after that encounter: "What a tragedy. He is a shadow of his former self."

A shadow of a man.

A man caught between darkness and light.

Sometimes it feels impossible to live from a full heart in times like these. But getting a clear view of what we *don't* want can be a first step toward positive action.

We don't want to become a cautionary tale.

We don't want to screw up, and we don't want to
    shut down.

We don't want apathy to creep in and darken our vision.

We don't want a faith that seems distant and irrelevant.

We don't want to serve a distorted vision of success that
    damages those we love.

We don't want to overreact and become a cliché of a man.

We don't want to abandon the Bible for the sake of fitting in
    and avoiding controversy.

And yet, many men today are doing these things, the very things we don't want to do. Under the constant pressure, we find ourselves becoming what we don't want to be. Why do we leave the light and drift into the darkness?

### Running to the Shadows

Very few men today feel prepared for the challenges we face or the complexities of our times. Perhaps our fathers were unaware of the guidance we needed or lacked the skill to impart it. They were probably dealing with their own wounds and trauma. We rarely encounter grown men today who were properly initiated as teenage boys—a significant and intentional process shared by almost all cultures, past and present, beyond the modern Western world we live in today.

School didn't seem to help us much either. For many of us, school felt like it was more about social climbing and connecting than preparation for real life. Further, multiple studies show boys generally are not cut out for traditional classroom learning as much as girls, with learning styles that are at odds with the approaches favored in mass schooling. No wonder boys typically display far more disruptive behaviors in school.[2]

And what about the church? Unfortunately, much of what is taught at church about masculinity is so theoretical that it doesn't seem to work in real life. There are a multitude of expectations we simply cannot live up to. We are supposed to be leaders and servants, strong and sensitive, healthy and whole. We are meant to be emotionally available, sexually restrained, biblically literate, and theologically informed. But in the absence of effective mentors and models, not to mention the lack of margin to really work on ourselves, we just drift to the edge—out of the light, out of the pressure, and into the shadows where the expectations are low.

## *Hiding in the Shadows*

We have all done things we are ashamed of. We have sinned sexually and lied about it. We have all spent our money on frivolous things to fend off pain. We have failed to keep our commitments to people who deserve more from us. Some of us experienced abuse growing up—whether verbal, physical, or sexual—that has caused us to cope in ways we may now regret. Many have been faking it for years, standing in the light during the day, but coming home with a crippling sense of imposter syndrome, convinced in our hearts that we don't have what it takes. We feel like the Tin Man from *The Wizard of Oz*, lacking a heart and with nothing to give. We are terrified of being seen for who we truly are.[3]

## *Sinning in the Shadows*

These are days of depravity. It's like Romans 1 is happening in front of our eyes, a slow descent from God's good designs for our world into corruption.[4] And whether out of brokenness, curiosity, or just the evil inside, sometimes we choose the shadows. We are enticed by forbidden things, the things we can now access without being found out.

Many of us have hidden parts of ourselves, shadows within that we are scared to admit or scared to confront. For famed psychoanalyst Carl Jung, the shadow referred to the things we repress. This would include our unacknowledged impulses, desires, and fears, made up of the parts of ourselves that we have disowned, denied, or rejected because they don't fit with our conscious self-image or the social norms and expectations. And there are times, when desire is strong, that we explore what has been lurking there all along.

### Secrets in the Shadows

A famous maxim states, "We are as sick as our secrets." All of us have secrets that hold us hostage, things that cause terror at the thought of being found out. Maybe your secret is a family secret, something that happened when you were growing up that you refuse to acknowledge. Maybe it is a moral secret, something from adolescence that haunts you to this day. Maybe it is a personal secret, shame about your body or your sexuality that you keep in the dark.

Are there things you are hiding that keep you from the light? Things you will never share for fear of rejection and ridicule?

## YOU WERE BORN FOR THE LIGHT

But here's the absolute truth: you were not born for the shadows; you were born for the light.

And as men we are called to be ruthless in our effort to get in—and *stay* in—the light. God did not create you to crawl through life crippled by anxiety and angst. Jesus did not die so that you could shrink back in shame. God did not send his Spirit to your heart to cry "imposter!"

The commission of heaven has not been given so you can be a domesticated, unhealthy, anemic shadow of a man.

So stop chasing and living in the shadows. It leads to decay and darkness.

Think about it: What do shadows do? They lurk. They

> As men we are called to be ruthless in our effort to get in—and *stay* in—the light.

are constantly with you. You can't escape them. They *follow* you. But they are also silent. They are subtle. If you are busy enough and distracted enough, you'll forget they exist.

They are pure darkness. They are the absence of light.

And when you try to fight them, you discover that they are elusive. You find yourself punching at nothing.

That's what it feels like to be a man today. There are many different shadows over us, on us, and within us. They are quiet, but they are killing us. They loom large and stick to us wherever we go. Do you recognize these shadows? Do you yearn to step into the light? If any part of your heart recognizes the struggle we're talking about—the angst, the confusion, the sense of paralysis—be encouraged.

You are not alone in this battle.

There is a way out of the shadows.

You can step into the light.

But to get there, you'll need a little defiance—like Diogenes. He wouldn't allow *anything* to get in the way of his light, not even the world's most powerful monarch. Light heals us and transforms us, but we must fight to stay in its radiance.

## STEP INTO THE LIGHT

For many years, we have been walking with men out of the shadows into the light. We have been unmasking the lies, starving out the strongholds, and going after friends who have gotten lost along the way. And that's the journey we want to take with you.

In our time together we are going to expose the source of the shadows falling over your heart. We are going to confront what's been lurking in the shadows of your story, heal what's been hiding out of shame, and summon what's been cowering out of fear.

You are going to fight the shadows of shame and despair that seek to rob you of confidence and hope. You are going to fight the shadows of loneliness and lust that keep you isolated and afraid. And you are going to fight the shadows of futility, apathy, and ambition that seek to rob you of faith and reduce your passion to passivity and compliance.

You are also going to see God do a real work of redemption. Some of the things you have been ashamed of will become places of strength. Some of your greatest failures will become the most potent lessons. Some of your deepest wounds will become your deepest source of wonder.

Robert Bly wrote, "Where a man's wound is, that is where his genius will be. Wherever the wound appears in our psyches, whether from alcoholic father, shaming mother, shaming father, abusing mother, whether it stems from isolation, disability, or disease, that is precisely the place for which we will give our major gift to the community."[5]

The community of men needs your gifts. They need your story of redemption. They need your authenticity, your energy, *you*.

And God is going to show up in surprising and powerful ways. He will walk with you through the valley of the shadow of death, and the promise of the coming of Jesus is the promise of light.

Facing your shadows feels like death. But you don't get resurrection light without the cross of death. As Matthew 4:16 reminds us, "The people who were sitting in darkness saw a great Light, and those who were sitting in the land and shadow of death, upon them a Light dawned" (NASB).

Light is on the horizon.

# CHAPTER 01

# THE
# ECLIPSE

**It's August 11, 2018, and I (Jon) am standing on** top of a building in New York City. I am looking up through a pair of carefully rigged glasses to observe what appears to be a physical impossibility.

The sun is disappearing before my eyes.

I blink repeatedly to try to adjust to what is happening. From my vantage point on Forty-Fifth and Ninth in the middle of Manhattan, something seems bigger than the sun.

The sun is being swallowed by the moon. If I were living a thousand years ago, I might have thought this was the apocalypse. It might have felt like the end had come. *What terrible power could block out the light of the sun?* Even with the knowledge that an eclipse is a natural (and temporary) phenomenon, it's a surreal experience to sit in the shadow of a complete eclipse.

But I know the end hasn't come, and that in a few minutes the world will return to normal. The sun is as powerful as ever, but from my limited vantage point on earth, it appears as though the sun has been snuffed out. Something came between the sun and me and distorted reality.

As it turns out, the source of many of our struggles comes from another kind of eclipse.

## FRAGILE FAITH

In Luke 22 we are let in on one of the most startling conversations in redemptive history. It was a conversation between Jesus and Satan, and it was regarding Peter's faith. Jesus said, "Simon, Simon, Satan has asked to sift all of you as wheat. But I have prayed for you, Simon, that your faith may not fail. And when you have turned back, strengthen your brothers" (vv. 31–32).

This is not the kind of revelation you want to hear from Jesus. Why couldn't he just rebuke Satan on Peter's behalf? Why couldn't Jesus remove the attack? Why couldn't he let Peter live in peace?

But we see a clue in this passage that has massive implications for you as a man. Satan overplayed his hand in his conversation with Jesus. He revealed his goal and his strategy for our lives. The clue is in the word *fail*. Satan was seeking to see Peter fail. Jesus was praying for him not to.

Here is the heart of the battle: we hate to fail as men. Much of the pain we face arises from the sense of failure in our hearts. We feel like we have failed in our faith, doubting God, and disobeying his Word. We feel like failures at work, torn by ambition, frustration, and apathy. We feel like failures with women, not understanding how to love and respect them, while being tempted to use and commodify them. We feel like failures with our kids, getting snappy and bored at the same time.

Satan's vision is for you to fail. Satan is at war to make sure you do. He is working toward the demise of men.

But failure is not just his goal, it is his strategy. The Greek word for *fail* is ekleip , and it has the same root as the English word *eclipse*, with the idea that during an eclipse the light fails. When something comes between the light and us, it casts a shadow over us, and we scramble in the dark. In fact, Luke used this same Greek word to describe what happened when Jesus was on the cross.

> It was now about noon, and darkness came over the whole land
> until three in the afternoon, for the sun stopped shining. And
> the curtain of the temple was torn in two. (Luke 23:44–45)

The sun was still there, but something blocked the light. An eclipse had occurred. Satan's plan is to position something between you and God so that you cannot see his light. He wants the shadow of this substitute to fall over your life. He wants you to think that God is gone, the problem is all there is, and you are destined to struggle in the dark. Satan wants you to fail. Satan's strategy is to eclipse God's presence with problems and temptations by bringing

**Satan's plan is to position something between you and God so that you cannot see his light.**

5

them so close to your face that you cannot see beyond them. He wants to distort your vision and bend your reality so that God disappears behind the temptation in front of you.

## THE STRENGTH OF THE SHADOW

Satan's strategy may seem simple, but he has perfected it through countless generations of men. He knows that when we can see God with clarity, we can resist temptation and move forward. But if he can block us from the light, the shadows will fall and our faith will flounder. The Scriptures are full of accounts like this.

Consider Peter, one of Jesus' most devoted disciples. He was a part of Jesus' inner circle. Peter saw Jesus raise people from the dead, exercise power over nature, and cast out demons. He witnessed Jesus in his splendor on the Mount of Transfiguration. He was granted insight into Jesus' true identity and invited to the place of secret prayer. Yet, Peter ended up denying Jesus three times in one night and running back to his nets, returning to his old life as a fisherman after Jesus' death—even though Jesus had warned Peter and prepared him for that difficult time (Luke 22:54–62).

How could Peter turn back after seeing so much light? An eclipse. Satan positioned something between Jesus and Peter to distort his vision. He couldn't understand the purposes of God and felt like all was lost. His fear eclipsed his faith, and he stumbled back. Ashamed of his inability to keep his own word, he went back to fishing. The shadows can lead us to do unthinkable things.

Think about the Israelites in the wilderness. God had delivered them through a series of stunning miracles, triumphing over the power of the Egyptian gods and the military might of Pharaoh. Yet when it came time to enter the promised land, they faltered. Their vision was distorted. Instead of seeing the power and promises of God, they saw the size of the inhabitants of the land God had promised to give them. They looked with fear and doubt at the Canaanites' walled cities.

The challenges loomed so large they blocked out the Israelites' vision of God and a shadow of fear fell over their hearts. Listen to how Scripture describes the Israelites' warped perspective as their fears of the powerful Canaanites eclipsed God: "We seemed like grasshoppers in our own eyes, and we looked the same to them" (Numbers 13:33). The first generation that was delivered from slavery in Egypt would never see the land they longed for. Most would perish in the wilderness.

Or think about David's failure, despite all God had done for him. He had been pulled out of obscurity to national prominence with the defeat of Goliath and handed the kingdom in the kindness of God. David had riches and power and fame. He knew those blessings came from God and was zealous for God's Word and his will. Yet, when he saw a woman from the roof, all perspective disappeared (2 Samuel 11:1–27).

Zeal for God's presence was gone, loyalty to the law was gone, the beauty of God was drowned out by the beauty of the woman. The light to his feet and lamp to his path was extinguished by his passion, and the shadow of sin fell over his heart. Abusing his power and taking advantage of the woman, David allowed the light of God to be blocked out by the shadow of lust.

This shadow would linger over David's life all his days and cause havoc in his family for generations to come. The shadow of lust took out a man after God's own heart.

> The shadow of lust took out a man after God's own heart.

Satan wants what happened to Peter, the Israelites, and David to happen to you. He wants to put things in front of your face so that the shadows of fear and temptation block out the light of God. He wants to distort your vision so your faith fails and you feel like you might as well give up. He wants to rob you of life, rub your face in your mistakes, and paralyze you with shame. He may even have had some success so far.

But take heart, hope is not lost. In the coming pages we are going to reposition your eyes so you can see past the eclipse, back to the source of light that frees you from failure and shame and lets you hold your head high with confident trust. God can even use your points of failure as a place of ministry, learning to strengthen your brothers as you regain your footing and begin to move toward the light.

## FIGHTING IN THE SHADE

The movie *300* tells the account of the Battle of Thermopylae in the Greco-Persian Wars. King Leonidas led three hundred of his elite Spartan soldiers against the Persian king Xerxes. Xerxes' 300,000 men jumped off the boats like a tsunami of violence breaking on the Grecian shore. Xerxes sent a message to the

Spartans to surrender, as their cause was futile. He warned them he was about to rain down terror and violence like they had never seen, boasting "our arrows will blot out the sun."

The Spartans, not intimidated in the least, replied, "Then we will fight in the shade."[1]

In one of history's most compelling battles, the Spartans, outnumbered in men and weapons, held the Persians at bay and fought with such heroic force that their story has echoed through the ages of history and inspired countless generations of men.

Satan is sifting the men of this generation with violent force. And he wants to sift you. His plan is to send wave after wave of attack against you to blot out the sun. But take heart, we are going to learn to fight in the shade.

**Take heart, we are going to learn to fight in the shade.**

## DIAGNOSING THE SHADOWS

The shadows we're talking about in this book derive their power from an illusion—no matter the fear or the failure that seems to be eclipsing the light, the light is still there. But, if you will allow us to mix metaphors for a moment, the symptoms of the shadows are very real. When the eclipse is all you can see, sickness sets in.

And I can tell you that one of the hardest things to bear in life is sickness without a cure.

I (Jeff) went through a long period of sickness recently that robbed me of energy and power. It was gut-wrenching to feel like a spectator in my own family, to lack the capacity to fully engage with my kids, to struggle with the challenge to live my calling at work, to be present with my wife, Alyssa. She cried about it almost weekly. And there was nothing I could do.

Like a typical man, I tried to power through it in the early days, thinking it was just a cold or the flu. But after my tenth night in a row with chills that made my teeth chatter so hard they nearly broke, losing pounds of water each night in sweat, barely able to open my eyes during the day because of the pain, and a golf-ball-sized lump developing in my thigh, I knew something was really wrong. I dragged myself to an ER.

That began a deeply frustrating and demoralizing process of visiting doctor after doctor who couldn't seem to get at the root of what was happening.

The revolving door of diagnoses and prescriptions felt like whiplash. Nothing seemed to work, and some of the supposed solutions made things worse.

Weirdly, a few months in, my illness began to affect my breathing. I couldn't take in a full breath. One time, it got to the point where I had to drive to the emergency room as fast as I could, gasping for breath as I drove. And let me tell you, that was *scary*. When breathing becomes that hard, you feel like you are dying. Watching your kids and wife see you in a state like that is a whole nother level of weakness and vulnerability.

It was the hardest year of my life. And the truth is, the physical pain wasn't even the worst part. The lack of answers, the feeling of powerlessness, and the sheer amount of time I was sick began to degrade my spirit.

I went through a battery of tests, but no answers came, and I kept getting worse. The doctors' language began getting more intense, their tone more somber, and I entered a state of deep discouragement.

You can imagine the sheer relief when a diagnosis finally came through. This was a lesson on "not all doctors are created equal" because after seeing multiple specialists, getting multiple scans, and googling my symptoms for dozens of hours, one lung specialist was able to pinpoint what was wrong within forty-five seconds of seeing me—wild. Turns out I had a super-rare lung infection that, coupled with my history of asthma, had created a scenario where my immune system was attacking my lungs.

Maybe it is the fact we live on Maui, where everyone is pretty "crunchy" (organic, nontoxic-living vibes), but my first jump typically isn't to pharmaceuticals. This specialist prescribed me something, and when I say I was jarringly better in *five minutes*, I am not exaggerating. It was one of the more surreal experiences of my life.

My ordeal ended up lasting eighteen months, from the onset of symptoms to the diagnosis and successful treatment. Looking back, that feels pretty quick, a blip on the timeline. But it felt like an eternity when I was in the thick of it and didn't have answers.

I never want to forget that eighteen-month darkness I went through—the pain, the feeling of dependence, and what it did to my spirit. It changed me.

It taught me the power of finding the right doctor who can make the right diagnosis and offer the right solution.

Before jumping into the rest of this book—naming the shadows, dismantling lies that empower them, and focusing on the truths that will set you free—I want to reassure you about the diagnosis we're offering. Many men feel the same kind of emotional, mental, and spiritual pain I did during that year and a half of undiagnosed illness—feeling paralyzed and powerless as they try to understand what is wrong with their lives and their hearts.

And there's no shortage of voices claiming to know why men are failing and what to do about it.

Many sociologists tell us our traditional values are outdated and harmful for the society we live in now.

Many activists tell us masculinity is a social construct and the deep urge we men have within ourselves to use our strength and capacity is nothing more than the clinging vestiges of the patriarchy refusing to let go of control.

Many progressives within the church often join the world's chorus, telling us God has done away with gender and we are free to define ourselves by a subjective, personal, internal compass.

I don't know about you, but none of the advice the culture is giving rings true about the roots of my struggles or depths of longing.

Our world today doesn't have the necessary paradigms to address the core needs of our hearts. These diagnoses may reveal something about the brokenness of men but not the design of men. They reveal some of what has gone wrong but can't even agree if there is such a thing as right.

To sit before these experts and subject yourself to the scrutiny of their critique isn't going to provide you with a vision of how to move forward or become whole. And that's because secular culture has removed the paradigm of creation, design, and purpose that defines who we truly are.

So let's get a few things clear:

The world can't tell you how to be a man because it can't even define what a man is.

The world can't tell you how to be a man because it doesn't believe there is an original intent for what man was created to be.

The world can't tell you how to be a man because most of the failures of men were simply men doing what the culture told them to do in their time.

Without some deeper, grounding truth, how can we discern whether the latest messages of our culture are true or setting us up for untold damage—in the present and for future generations?

It's not that the world doesn't have things to say to the problems men face today; it's that it can't say *enough*. It can't touch the depth of brokenness caused by sin or bring the hope of salvation to bear on our wounds. God's diagnosis is a gift, even if a painful one. It's the only way to get the healing we need.

Let's start fighting these shadows together—naming them, identifying the lie that gives them power, and dragging every shadowed part of our hearts into the life-giving light of God's trustworthy, truthful diagnosis.

# THE SHADOW OF DESPAIR

*The Lie:* There is nothing really worth living for.

*The Truth:* Your hope is secure in Jesus.

**The *Back to the Future* movies are far and away** the best films about time travel.

*Twelve Monkeys* and *Looper* are tied for second, but they are a *distant* second.

But one thing that is true of most time-travel movies is if anyone goes back into the past, people in that past timeline can tell.

The people from the future are *different.*

Remember how everyone from 1955 thought Michael J. Fox's character, Marty McFly, was wearing a life jacket? He was wearing a red puffy vest—pretty standard attire for 1985. But thirty years into the past? Not so much.

In a more serious moment from that film, a black employee at a diner in 1955 says he's going to be the mayor of the town someday. Such an idea was unthinkable to his boss. But we as the audience know that in 1985, his hope is a reality. He does, in fact, become the mayor.

There's an important lesson there. Hope and despair are all about how *we see the future and what we believe about it*. And genuine biblical hope is rooted in what we believe about the future and how we concretely let it affect our present.

Those without hope have a misinformed or blocked view of the future, which poisons their present. For the boss at the diner, he couldn't even imagine a world in which an African American could be mayor—because he couldn't imagine a future that was all that different from the present.

> Hope and despair are all about how we see the future and what we believe about it.

Many men are in a state of massive despair because they have forgotten their future—their inheritance, their calling, their horizon. They only see the present, and the bleakness of the present seeps into their hearts, a shadow that robs life of its possibilities.

## DYING FROM DESPAIR

There is so much despair among men today that we have a mortality category for it: "deaths of despair," which include deaths by suicide, accidental drug overdoses, and complications of alcoholism. These types of deaths disproportionately affect men. Depending on the age range, men are anywhere from *four to nearly ten times* more likely than women to experience a death of despair.[1] Men are killing themselves, "sometimes slowly over the course of their lifetime or abruptly through impulsive risk-taking, violent encounters, and suicide."[2]

The Brookings Institute, a widely respected think tank, put together a dire report on the problem titled *Addressing America's Crisis of Despair and Economic Recovery: A Call for a Coordinated Effort*. Their conclusion? "There is the need for a new federal inter-agency task force to coordinate existing and new efforts to address addiction, despair, and economic recovery as a critical first step."[3] In other words, the problem is so serious, according to this think tank's assessment, that they thought we should stop at nothing short of massive intervention by the government.

But you know what's not very popular right now? Any program, task force, or airtime given to men and their problems.

A recent *Washington Post* article on the problems facing men today notes, "Many assume they're doing fine and bristle at male complaint" but "the data show it, [and] so does the general mood: Men find themselves lonely, depressed, anxious and directionless."[4]

What can we do about it? How do we crawl out of the hole of despair in which we find ourselves?

## OPTIMISM WON'T GET YOU THERE

I'll (Jeff) tell you one thing that won't solve the problem: telling ourselves to *just be optimistic*.

Optimism is basically what I like to call worldly hope. It's not concrete. It has no surety. It's wishful thinking that says, "Maybe my future will be different." It's deficient.

But even though it's not a full-blown solution, optimism is not such a bad place to start. Optimism alone has been found to have some benefits.

In fact, there's a lot of research around this. People with optimistic attitudes about life show themselves to have higher levels of well-being and life satisfaction, stronger levels of resilience in the face of difficulties, and improved mental health. They also have much better physical health, including lower levels of inflammation, better cardiovascular health, and being less prone to chronic illness.[5]

That is stunning to me. Those are serious benefits.

But maybe we shouldn't be surprised. The war is in the mind. It starts there. And more men need to do war in the mind so they can win the war in the world. Our thoughts become actions, our actions become behaviors, and our behaviors become our lives.

We would do well to take our thoughts seriously. An optimistic outlook is a great place to start. But mere optimism is no substitute for hope.

## WISHES VERSUS EXPECTATION

While optimism is little more than wishful thinking, hope operates at another level. Hope at its essence is about *expectation*.

The reason so many men think they don't have any control over their present is because they don't have any expectation about their future. They see life as something that is happening to them. And when you live without expectation, despair is just around the corner. But let me tell you right now, brothers—despair is evil.

THE SHADOW OF DESPAIR

It's from the Enemy. It's a poison. And you have to go after it, or else it will kill you.

Let's conduct a thought experiment. Two guys are both tasked with working a tough manual-labor job every single day, with no days off, for one entire year. That would be grueling, right? Now let's say one of those men was promised $10 million when he completed the year of work, while the other man was promised just $10,000.

**The reason so many men think they don't have any control over their present is because they don't have any expectation about their future.**

Can we agree that these two men would have wildly different approaches to the work? Different levels of grit? Different spirits? Just a few weeks in, I imagine one of these men would start to get grumpy, to hate his life, to despair.

But the guy who is expecting $10 million? Even though the work is just as backbreaking as the other guy's, I can imagine him doing it with a smile on his face, thinking, *Every day is one day closer to $10 million.*

Here's the obvious truth. For the guy expecting to become a multimillionaire, the promise and blessing of the future far outweighs the pain of the present. How you experience the present is dictated by your belief about the future. How you live now is determined by how you believe you will live then.

## UNMET HOPE

Viktor Frankl, who wrote *Man's Search for Meaning*, had so many insights on hope and despair from his time in Nazi concentration camps during World War II. He observed that "if a prisoner lost faith in his future, he was doomed."[6] Frankl told a story of Felix, a fellow inmate in the concentration camp. Felix had a dream in which a voice told him he could wish for anything, so he wished to know when they would be liberated from the concentration camp.

That voice whispered March 30, and Felix believed it.

*He gave that voice authority.*

*He was convinced they'd be free by March 30.*

But as the date got closer, they were still in the camps. March 29 came. Felix started to question his expectation. March 30 arrived with no freedom in sight and Felix fell seriously ill. On March 31, Felix died.

He died from a wrong belief in the future. His body shut down in response to his brain's losing hope. A loss of hope killed him:

> The ultimate cause of my friend's death was that the expected liberation did not come and he was severely disappointed. This sudden load on his body's resistance to disease gave way. His faith in the future and his will to live had become paralyzed and his body fell victim to illness and thus the voice of his dream was right.[7]

Frankl went on to note that the concentration camps saw a disproportionate number of deaths around Christmas time for the exact same reason. Robert Kishaba, writing for the Museum of Jewish Heritage, summed up Frankl's observations:

> Between Christmas 1944 and New Year's 1945 the camp's sick ward experienced a death rate "beyond all previous

experience," not due to a food shortage or worse living conditions, but because, "the majority of the prisoners had lived in the naïve hope that they would be home again by Christmas." When this hope was unmet, prisoners found no reason to continue holding on, nothing to look forward to. When a mind lets go, so does its body.[8]

## GET YOUR TELOS RIGHT

One of the most important things for every man is getting your *telos* right.

What's *telos*? It's a Greek word that can be translated as "chief aim." In other words, if your life is an arrow, where is it pointed? That's your telos. And whether you like it or not, your telos dominates how you live. It fuels everything.

But you have to get your telos right, or it won't do you any good in the long run. Like Felix in the concentration camp, if your telos is wrapped up in an unfounded hope, you'll just be taking the long way around to despair.

Maybe you think your telos is to become rich. But if that isn't looking likely anytime soon?

*Despair.*

Maybe you think your telos is to be married and have kids and grandkids and a big family when you're older. But if you're single right now or divorced?

*Despair.*

Or maybe you think your telos is to be successful, but your professional life keeps getting derailed or running into dead ends.

*Despair.*

Holding on to a faulty or insufficient telos is a path to despair. Remember, a telos is not just any aim, but your *chief* aim. The ultimate purpose that your life is pointed at.

We see our true telos in Scripture. God is making all things new, repairing and renewing all the broken and dead parts around us—*and he asks us to partner with him*. What an ask! The calling we have in the here and now is wrapped up in the future God has planned in Christ. One day, because of the resurrection of Jesus, we know the work of total restoration will be complete. Every warped and broken thing in this world is being redeemed.

Now, that is a telos worth aiming for.

Here's where things get interesting. Our telos isn't something we can create just by thinking about it. It has to work itself down into our desires and cravings. It has to go from conscious thinking *to a primal longing embedded in us*. James K. A. Smith put it this way: "But the telos we live toward is not something we primarily know or believe or think about; rather, our telos is what we want, what we long for, what we crave."[9]

And that starts with first staring our misplaced hopes in the face—those aims that lead to despair—and calling them for what they are: lies.

## FALSE HOPES

Let me ask you this: What do you daydream about? What do you find yourself drifting toward in your thoughts? Answering those questions honestly tends to smoke out our false hopes.

So let's talk about three major false hopes that tend to show up in a man's life, particularly in a Christian man's life.

The first, *a disembodied heaven*. This might not sound like an obvious first choice, but for anyone following Jesus this is a misstep that is all too common in evangelical spheres, and it really is detrimental to our lives. We tend to believe or feel, without giving it much thought, that heaven is this far and distant place in the sky where our spirits go when we die. And we just kind of float around on clouds in an ethereal way.

But that is not the worldview of the Scriptures or first-century followers of Jesus. Heaven and earth in the Bible are described as overlapping realms, like when Jesus instructed his disciples to pray that God's will and rule would become a reality "on earth as it is in heaven" (Matthew 6:10). Does your telos involve heaven coming to earth, right now and in your daily life? It should.

Second, the hope of *no earthly suffering*. The reality is life is hard. We get sick. Our kids get sick. People around us die. We lose the house. Our business files for bankruptcy. We get fired. We make a few small wrong decisions and live with a life of regret.

The absence of earthly suffering is not our ultimate hope. Rather, our hope is that we aren't alone when we suffer and that earthly suffering isn't the end of the story. We worship a God who knows what it's like to suffer. And not only can he empathize, but he is actively doing something about it—using it for good and putting the world back together one moment at a time.

Third, we hope for *total control*. This is such a temptation for men. We hope that if we can just work enough, try enough, pursue enough, we can eventually have things "under control." But we aren't in control—and life will teach us that quickly. We can certainly suggest. Nudge. Push in a direction. But total control is an illusion. Our hope isn't in control. It's in the one who has control.

## HOPE BEYOND DESPAIR

Let me ask you something I want you to think about deeply: What is one promise God has made to you but has not kept?

There are no unkept promises with God.

In every other area of life, that type of certainty would shape us deeply, wouldn't it? Pause on this for a second. What have been the moments in your life when you've most felt despair? What areas of your heart and story does despair touch? Can you trace a misplaced hope behind it? A hope that is cheaper and lesser than our truest hope? And can you renounce that false hope right now?

Renouncing false hope is just the first step. You need to replace it with some promises and true hope from God Almighty. Here are a few to get you started.

- *Hope changes how we see suffering.* "Our light and momentary troubles are achieving for us an eternal glory that far outweighs them all" (2 Corinthians 4:17).
- *Hope changes how we see our daily work.* "We are . . . created in Christ Jesus for good works" (Ephesians 2:10 NASB).
- *Hope makes us bolder.* We are already "seated . . . in the heavenly realms in Christ Jesus" (Ephesians 2:6). Nothing can harm us.

- *Hope fills our hearts with praise.* "As for me, I will always have hope; I will praise you more and more" (Psalm 71:14).
- *Hope produces fruits of the Spirit.* "May the God of hope fill you with all joy and peace" (Romans 15:13).

Let me give you a quick two-part exercise that changed my life. I want you to run through it right now before moving on. I call it a hope log.

## Hope Log

1. Audit your adult years. Can you mark any moments where your view of (and hope for) the future changed the course of your life, whether for good or bad? Try to come up with five.
2. Create a plan to mark every moment throughout this next week where God's promised future of glory, goodness, and resurrected life enters your thoughts. I want you to see how often or seldom you allow God's good future to make its way into your daily life.

## MEN FROM THE FUTURE

Let's end this chapter with Jesus and the amazing thing he accomplished. He did what no one expected him to do: rip the future into the present. He threw a lasso around our future hope and said, "I think we should begin to experience that today. Right now."

What do I mean by that? In the first century, many Orthodox Jews believed in the resurrection of the dead. That part wasn't that crazy to many of them. But they all assumed it was going to happen *at the end of time.* There were two very distinct ages: the present age and the age to come. And the age to come was somewhere down there on the timeline. It was going to happen in a distant future.

But Jesus? He said the age to come was beginning in the present. That was radical.

Jesus' resurrection was not only proof of the future possibility of our resurrection, but a deposit, a down payment for that future inheritance. It's as if the future goodness, beauty, blessing, and glory that God has in store for us is beginning to surprise and meet us here in this present moment. Bible scholar N. T. Wright put it like this: "The hope is that God will eventually do for the whole creation what he did for Jesus; God is at work in the present, by the Spirit of Jesus, to prepare the world for that great remaking, that great unveiling (that great apocalypse, in fact) of the future plan."[10]

We need men from the future. In this sin-warped world, despair casts a long shadow and lurks at the edges of every man's hopes and dreams. But men who are living today in the light of the resurrection and God's good plan to restore all things—those are the kind of men who overcome the shadow of despair.

Your workplace needs more men from the future.

Your wife needs a husband from the future.

Your kids need a dad from the future.

Your friends need a man from the future.

Your neighbors need a man from the future.

The world needs more men from the future.

The resurrection wasn't an aberration; it was the first step toward the new normal. And that is our truest hope. So men, straighten your spines. Stand up tall. Raise your chins. Step out of the shadow of despair into the light of hope.

Let's end this chapter with a visual. Imagine you're in a big battle, sword in hand. You're on the front lines and you're fighting the enemy alongside a small band of brothers. You are part of a bigger army, but for the moment it's just you and this small group, facing overwhelming odds.

You are getting tired, and the specter of defeat looms larger by the minute.

But then you notice the sound of footsteps behind you, quiet at first but gradually

> Step out of the shadow of despair into the light of hope.

growing to a deafening roar. The rest of your brothers are on the way. You hear a trumpet and recognize it as the rallying call for your army.

You know now that help is on the way. Its arrival is imminent.

What do you think that would do to the sword in your hand? What do you think that would do to your weary legs? That stampede of horses and brothers coming over the crest of the hill would give you a shot of hope and energy that would immediately translate to how you're fighting the battle.

Has help arrived? Are the reinforcements on the front lines with you quite yet?

No.

But help is on the way and hope is on the horizon. That future hope changes you in the present moment. And so it is with us as men and Jesus. We know our future. Help is on the way. The armies of heaven are rising over the crest. Do not give up the battle. Hold your head high and your sword higher. You are backed by legions in the spiritual realm, and they are moving toward you. Let that quicken your spirit today.

# THE SHADOW OF LONELINESS

*The Lie:* Loneliness is part of being a man.

*The Truth:* Friendship is a superpower.

## "I can't feel *anything.*"

I (Jeff) said this to my wife last year over a ten-minute morning coffee check-in at our kitchen island.

As I was fumbling over saying how I felt out loud, I said, "I don't know what it is, I just feel dead. I don't feel joy, but I don't feel deep, aching sadness either. I just don't . . . *feel.*"

It had taken me a few months to admit something so simple.

It felt like a deep, deep fog was over my mind and spirit. And simply put, *I wasn't doing well.*

But it wasn't *nothing.* Whatever it was, I knew if I stayed on that path, my spirit would slowly decompose. It felt like my spiritual Check Engine light had been on the last few months and that if I didn't get a checkup soon it could get serious.

Dead people slowly decay—wither. They have no feelings.

That's what it felt like.

And here's the kicker that made it especially tough: judging by external circumstances, I was doing better than ever. I'd worked tirelessly for years to get a few business things off the ground, and they finally were thriving. And after pouring myself into parenting during my kids' younger years, which sometimes felt like a journey that would never end, that effort was bearing small, incremental fruit as well. It felt like we'd finally crossed the first checkpoint of family health we'd been waiting for: the kids loved each other, worked together, seemed healthily attached to my wife and me—of course they still punched each other in the face from time to time, but we don't need to talk about that, you know what I mean.

Things weren't perfect, but *they were good*. And that's something I hadn't been able to say in every season of the past decade.

But while things seemed good, I felt like I was beginning to lose touch. It felt like a slow fade, for reasons I couldn't quite pinpoint. I just knew I was sad and numb. I felt like a zombie. My wife, Alyssa, noticed and felt the effects too.

I wanted my heart back.

I didn't know where it had gone. But I didn't have it anymore and I wanted it back.

That's when my wife asked a pointed question: "Don't answer right away—think on it for a second. When was the last time you felt genuinely full and alive and joyful?"

A few brief moments in the last decade came to mind, certainly some moments in marriage and parenting.

But the answer that surprised me the most and came into my head almost immediately was *college*. Young adulthood, when I was twenty to twenty-two years old.

Why?

Friends.

I had friends.

Deep, rich, life-giving, energetic friendships.

I lived with eleven guys at the time. We were paying $200 in rent, and I had a basement bedroom with six-and-a-half-foot ceilings. We made our own bunk beds out of some plywood and 2x4s because of the low ceilings. And even with the DIY bunk beds it was still tight—so tight in fact that we had to slip my friend into his top bunk every night like a pizza coming off a pizza peel.

We were sharing deep dreams, working on projects together. But most of all we were sharing hearts. Brothers in the trenches. I remember crying with some of those guys over tough relationship stuff and over our struggles with sin that entangled us. We shared everything—the highs, the lows, the joys, and the sadness.

*Brothers.*

A few days after I shared that with Alyssa, one of those friends called me.

The busyness of life had captured both of us, and what used to be daily conversations when we were roommates had turned into weeks and then months between check-ins. We were still close, but there was no proximity and no unplanned interaction.

As soon as I picked up the phone and heard the deep sadness in my friend's voice, I knew something was wrong. "Hey man," he said, "I need to tell you something. I've been dating this girl, and yesterday she came over and found some text messages and emails on my phone showing I've been going to illegal massage parlors for sex. She left in a rage—but before walking out she took pictures of the emails and texts and said if I don't pay her thousands

35

of dollars, she's going to send it to everyone I care about. So I'm calling you to tell you before she does. Also, I don't know what happened, man. I don't quite know how I got here in this moment."

Mind you, this is a guy who loves Jesus. He'd been a successful leader. He'd started and led ministries and discipled dozens, if not hundreds, of people.

"I'm so sorry, man," I said. "You must be feeling so much shame and weight right now."

He immediately started crying.

After chatting for more than an hour, I suggested mapping out the last few years of his life to figure out how he got there.

He immediately said, "Yeah, it feels like I've lost something since those days we were together in our twenties. I don't know what happened—I'm just so much lonelier. And I can feel it."

We had completely different trajectories since our twenties, completely different seasons and places we'd gotten to. *But we both felt lonely.*

It's hard to articulate just how it feels, but an apt metaphor would be all the colors draining out of your world. You gradually start seeing—and feeling—everything in black and white. But you have a wife, kids, responsibilities, a job to tend to—so much depends on you—so you don't stop to process or think about it. You just keep chugging along.

## UNWANTED SOLITUDE

A recent study revealed some interesting insights about the impact of loneliness.[1] A group of men was brought in and asked to fill out a brief personality questionnaire. Then, they were assigned to different feedback groups. But here's the catch—the participants thought they were assigned to groups based on the personality questionnaires they'd filled out, but they were divided up randomly. The three groups were the

- "future belonging" group,
- "future alone" group, and the
- "misfortune control" group.

The "future belonging" group was told after the questionnaire, "You're the type who has rewarding relationships throughout your life. You're likely to have a long and stable marriage and have friendships that last into your later years. The odds are that you'll always have friends and people who care about you."

The "future alone" group was told the opposite. "You're the type who will end up alone later in life. You may have friends and relationships now, but by your midtwenties most of these will have drifted away. You may even marry or have several marriages, but these are likely to be short-lived and not continue into your thirties. Relationships don't last, and when you're past the age where people are constantly forming new relationships, the odds are you'll end up being alone more and more."[2]

Finally, the "misfortune control" group was basically a control group to see if negative feedback in general affected the males, or just negative feedback specifically pertaining to their social isolation. They were told, "You're likely to be accident prone later in life—you might break an arm or a leg a few times, or maybe be

37

injured in car accidents. Even if you haven't been accident prone before, these things will show up later in life, and the odds are you will have a lot of accidents."[3]

The results were striking to the point it made me ask, *Are we really that impressionable?* The "future belonging" and "misfortune control" groups were basically unaffected by the feedback and showed no adverse consequences. But there were dramatic behavior changes in the "future alone" group. According to Joiner, "in the laboratory they engage in more aggressive behavior, less helpful behavior toward others, more self-defeating behavior. . . . [But] one thing 'future alone' participants tend *not* to display, very surprisingly, is negative mood or distress. Instead, their mood state is best characterized as 'numb.'"[4]

The negative feedback didn't make them observably grumpy or sad. Rather, the prospect of being doomed to loneliness essentially *froze and dulled them.*

And that's exactly what loneliness does. According to Joiner, loneliness is the "experience of unwanted solitude and disconnection."[5] Further, loneliness has two facets: *social isolation* and *emotional isolation*, with emotional loneliness being the symptom of the root of the problem—social isolation.

## DANGEROUSLY NUMB

The way loneliness affects people reminds me of Ashlyn Blocker. Ashlyn has what's called congenital insensitivity to pain (CIP). It's a rare genetic mutation, and as the name suggests, it prevents the person who has it from feeling pain. Being impervious to pain might seem like an advantage, a superpower of sorts. But it's enormously detrimental.

When Ashlyn was a young girl, she completely burned off the skin on the palm of her hand by placing it on a hot pressure washer—she didn't realize she was being burned until it was too late. She was once swarmed and bitten by hundreds of fire ants without realizing it. As a newborn she almost chewed off her entire tongue.[6]

Why?

People with CIP can't feel pain, so they don't realize when damaging things are happening to them, such as burning flesh, a broken bone, or serious internal infections. And because of this, most people with CIP die very young.

CIP is a perfect metaphor for men's hearts today. Our hearts are frozen and numb, and we don't realize something is life threatening to our core self until it's too late.

All too often, we reach a place where we can't feel *anything*. And at first glance we might think it's because we're strong, that it's a superpower to move through life without being over-whelmed by emotions. But the reality is that we are suffering and dying on the inside, and we are just too numb to realize it.

Some of you might be wondering, *Can loneliness really kill?*

The answer is yes. Loneliness can, in fact, be just as strong a predictor for illness and death as smoking, obesity, and high blood pressure. Sleep is also less restorative for those who are lonely. Loneliness weakens your immune system. It also increases the risk of dying of heart disease, cancer, and stroke.

> The reality is that we are suffering and dying on the inside, and we are just too numb to realize it.

The research on loneliness as it relates to mortality is especially staggering. In one meta-analysis (a study of other studies), researchers found that "data across 308,849 individuals, followed for an average of 7.5 years, indicate that individuals with adequate social relationships have a 50 percent greater likelihood of survival compared to those with poor or insufficient social relationships."[7]

Not only does it kill, it warps your view of reality. In one study, college students were given a backpack loaded with significant weight. They were then led to a steep hill and asked to estimate how steep the hill was. Everyone got the same backpack with the same weight, and each was asked to assess the same hill. But those who assessed the hill alone, without a group, guessed it was *significantly* steeper and longer than those assessing it with a friend or two. And for those who assessed the hill's steepness with people who they had been friends with for a long time, that optimism was amplified.[8]

I don't think "getting in touch with your feelings" is the cure to loneliness. Nor do I think group therapy is the answer.

Can those things be helpful? Of course.

The real cure for loneliness is friendship—deep, enriching, beautiful, long-term friendship.

> The real cure for loneliness is friendship—deep, enriching, beautiful, long-term friendship.

But many guys don't have many friends. Have you ever heard the joke that the reason men golf is because they are too afraid to ask each other to go on walks together? There's some truth in that. Maybe another way to put it is they don't know how to be a good friend.

## THE POWER OF FRIENDSHIP

Faced with the realization of my own loneliness, I started doing some research. I do this when I am facing a problem. I can't stop asking, *What's the solution?*

Is there an objective way to find friends, or at least to understand how people become friends? I wanted to understand, not just out of curiosity but because I looked around and realized I didn't have many friends. I had acquaintances and guys I could call in emergencies, but all my male friendships felt like they were on the wrong trajectory. Instead of getting richer and deeper over time, every friendship I had seemed to be getting more depleted with each passing year.

As it turns out, there is some robust research into friendship. One of the studies I found to be most compelling began in 1934 and is still going today, called the Harvard Study of Adult Development.[9]

Yes, you read that right—a study that has been going on for ninety years.

Researchers at Harvard created a combined group of Harvard graduates and low-income teenage boys in Boston, all of whom were willing to let the researchers track them *for their entire lives.* These researchers measured anything and everything—DNA samples, psychological problems, marriages, deaths, and so on. In fact, twenty-five of the men donated their brains to the program after they died.

The data has been rock solid in demonstrating one very specific thing, surprising even the team of researchers: strong relationships matter more than just about anything else. They affect outcomes for men's lives more than IQ, social class, and money. Of all the metrics these researchers have been tracking, relationships clearly and definitively have had the most bearing on the men's satisfaction levels.

Let's rephrase that in a more personal way for you.

As you think about the next twelve months in your life after reading this book, what do you see as the best use of your time?

Some might argue it would be spending energy toward the start-up phase of a business. Some might say focusing on physical health and exercise.

And of course, those kinds of things are important.

But the best use of your time in terms of how much it will impact your life—emotionally, physically, and spiritually—has been verifiably shown to be *investing in deepening your relationships*.

Dr. Robert Waldinger, director of the Harvard Study of Adult Development, and his collaborator, Dr. Marc Schulz, have coined an interesting term for the healthy relationships that make all the difference for people who hope to experience happiness and satisfaction in life: "social fitness."[10] It should be treated as, talked about, and invested in just like physical fitness. Relationships atrophy if they are not worked out. You must consistently invest in the relationships around you, or you will be at an increased risk of getting sick and even dying early.

The truth is most of us men aren't working out at all when it comes to social fitness. Our friendships have gone from ripped and toned in college to a collective dad bod and gut. And it's because we are trying to live off yesterday's work.

Another set of research I found compelling revealed the key ingredients that make friendships strong. There are three factors most researchers have agreed on:

- Proximity
- Unplanned interactions
- Vulnerability[11]

When I first saw these three, I did a double take. The first two seem so *light*, if that makes sense. Proximity (simply being near each other) and unplanned interactions (such as running into each other without a calendar invite)—are these really the biggest factors in developing strong relationships?

Yes, that *is* pretty much all it takes. And yet, most things in our culture fight against those simple but foundational ingredients for healthy friendships.

Think about our culture and the technological advancements we've achieved over the last fifty to seventy-five years. A lot of the large breakthroughs directly impede our ability to do these three things. Take the car, for example. What an achievement. But now we no longer walk. We are no longer limited to blocks and steps and small towns. We rarely think about anything needing to be "within walking distance."

The new world of car transportation fundamentally changed how we engage with one another. We don't *encounter* one another anymore. We drive past one another, often alone, on the way to work, the store, or church. As one author put it, we "grind along together anonymously, often in misery."[12]

Wendell Berry's thoughts on the difference between a path (walking) versus a road (driving) are worth spending some time with:

> A path is little more than a habit that comes with knowledge of a place. It is a sort of ritual of familiarity. It is not destructive. It is the perfect adaptation, through experience and familiarity, of movement to place; it obeys the natural contours; such obstacles as it meets it goes around. A road, on the other hand, even the most primitive road, embodies a resistance against the landscape. Its reason is not simply the necessity for movement, but haste. Its wish is to avoid contact with the landscape; it seeks so far as possible to go over the country, rather than through it; its aspiration, as we see clearly in the example of our modern freeways, is to be a bridge; its tendency is to translate place into space in order to traverse it with the least effort. It is destructive, seeking to remove or destroy all obstacles in its way. The primitive road advanced by the destruction of the forest; modern roads advance by the destruction of topography.[13]

## MASTERING THE ART OF THE HANG

This research on friendship, relationships, and loneliness struck me deeply. I took it very seriously, not just because of my own growing awareness of my loneliness, but also because of what I see in the men around me. I know a few older men who are incredibly lonely. I'm thinking of one in particular who has been divorced a few times, is now retired, and never really made an effort to invest in friendships over the course of his long adult life. And now? He's seventy years old and alone every night. Every. Single. Night.

I didn't want that to be my future.

So I shot out a text to every guy I was relatively close with who lived within twenty minutes of me.

> Hey guys. Saturday, my house, 7 pm. I'm firing up the hot tub, starting a fire, and will provide cigars and my homemade smash burgers. And more importantly, I'm going to pick one thoughtful question I want to guide the discussion the entire night. Would love to have you.

I invited fifteen guys. Fourteen showed up.

Now it's a quarterly tradition that has gone on for years, and I can honestly say it's one of my most life-giving practices. It fills my tank like nothing else. For one thing, it's a lot of fun. There's a fun new recipe or activity for every meetup. But more importantly, it does something for my soul. I feel seen—not alone—like I'm in a tribe of brothers. And let me tell you, a deep, deep trust has transpired over time within this group. Talk about vulnerability—some of the things we share and help each other through are incredibly personal or difficult. Relationship struggles, health scares, crises of faith, business failures—you name it, we've talked about it.

Along the way I've learned two principles I try to let guide these times and my friendships: create the hang in your own image and ask great questions.

45

### Create the Hang in Your Own Image

I *love* to cook. So I do that for the hangs. I love to smoke cigars and drink bourbon, so I do that. I love deep discussions about books we are reading and ideas we are wrestling with. I love heart-level processing—and I also kind of hate the football and hunting chats—but if you ever invite me to that type of hang, I will still happily tell you why the Seahawks are the greatest underperforming football dynasty in NFL history. And guess what? The hangs I host are not for everyone. But they are life-giving and sharpening, and they seem to have an extremely positive effect on the guys in the crew.

Maybe for you it *is* hunting or football or whatnot. Whatever it is, *do that*. Lead it. Go after it. Gather a tribe of brothers who are genuinely glad to spend time with one another and who enjoy the same kinds of activities.

One specific way I've practiced this principle is by centering fire. Give me a minute to explain. I've always loved fire. I'll never forget when the neighbors called the cops on me when I was home alone, around twelve years old. I was bored and thought it would be fun to light fireworks inside the fireplace. I thought this idea was both genius and safe. I didn't realize that it sounded like legitimate bombs were going off in our home as the fireworks bellowed up the chimney for our whole neighborhood to hear!

But in all seriousness, think about how a fire changes things. How strange would it sound to send a text to a group of guys that says, "Hey, men, everyone come over to my house and we'll sit in a circle and share our feelings"? That's a hard pass for most men.

But you add flames in the center of that circle? Not weird anymore. And next thing you know, you're sharing your heart.

There's some science to back this up. Socializing by sitting around a fire not only dates back thousands of years and across all civilizations but also has legitimate biological benefits, such as lowering blood pressure and calming our bodies. The effect is so powerful that even the sounds and visuals of a fire on a television can have almost the same impact.[14]

I believe so much in the power of firepits to bring men together that I've shipped hundred-pound firepits across the country to friends because I visualize what it will do to their backyards, who will gather, and the stories that will be shared. I'm like a firepit evangelist. If firepits aren't your thing or you don't have a place for one, figure out the alternative that works for you. The important thing is to create a hang that invites men into real community with one another.

### Ask Great Questions

Be careful that you don't simply splash around in the shallows when you gather. Go deep. Don't waste your time on talking about stuff that doesn't matter. It's too easy for men to stay on the surface. Have you heard that joke about the guy who goes golfing with a recently divorced buddy? When he returns home after hours of golfing with this grieving friend, his wife somberly asks, "How is he doing? Is he holding up okay?" To which the guy replies, "Huh? How should I know how he's doing? But he did just buy a new 9 iron!" Don't let that be your guys hang. You have to go deeper. We are in a war. Cut the banter.

As the leader and host of a hang—whether we're talking about a morning Bible study, a late-night gathering around a fire, or a hunting excursion—your job description is to be a good question asker.

47

With the guys' night I host, I want to go so deep I tend to pick only one really good question to guide our discussion—after the food, of course. Here are a few from this year's hangs.

- What's been the hardest thing about this year for you? And how do you feel like it's shaping you and forming you?
- What's something serious you're more passionate about than you were five years ago and something you're less passionate about than you were five years ago?
- What is one mistake you will never make again?
- Name two to three of the greatest years of your life and why, and name the two to three worst years of your life and why.
- If you could only watch one movie for the rest of your life, what would it be? (This was a nonserious question I tacked onto the end of the night, but it turned out to be epic. We broke it down into categories like comedy and drama, and before long it turned into a serious debate with all kinds of surprising insights.)

Don't underestimate how important it is to dig a little deeper during these conversations. My friend Annie Downs was over for dinner one evening when she said something I'll never forget. "In a lot of my conversations," she said, "I've tried this experiment of adding two words to the end of moments where someone shares something deep or personal with me."

"What two words?" I asked.

"*What else*," she replied.

*What else?* It assumes there is more. It's curious. It says *keep going.*

Annie said the real stuff is always behind the *what else?* Always. And from my own experiences with it, I can attest that it's a magical phrase.

There is dark and serious and vulnerable stuff behind the *what else?*

Men, shoot out a text. Fire up the fire (pun intended). Create a tribe of brothers—right now. Despite the looming shadow of loneliness and all the verifiable negative impacts it has on your physical, mental, emotional, and spiritual health, there's a simple solution: invest in relationships.

> Despite the looming shadow of loneliness and all the verifiable negative impacts it has on your physical, mental, emotional, and spiritual health, there's a simple solution: invest in relationships.

The greatest threat to your well-being may not be the next presidential election, the state of the global economy, or any number of other stressors and challenges you're likely focused on. The greatest threat may very well be that you will skim across the surface of your life and miss the ordinary wonder and magic happening in the most important and sacred relationships God has given you.

## STAYING PRESENT IN A WORLD OF SCREENS

In his remarkable book *Three Pieces of Glass: Why We Feel Lonely in a World Mediated by Screens*, Eric O. Jacobsen presents a simple idea with profound implications about the way we show up in our lives. Three pieces of glass have isolated us from those we love and contributed to the epidemic of loneliness many of us feel today—and we need to be aware of their effect on our daily lives.

According to Jacobsen, those three pieces of glass are

- the smartphone screen,
- the TV screen, and the
- the windshield.[15]

If you are looking for what's casting the shadow of loneliness over your heart, there's a good chance those three pieces of glass are involved—and they represent distraction, escapism, and commuting. These are true threats to the life of community and connection you long for—and were made for.

### The Smartphone Screen

According to Michael Easter in his book *The Comfort Crisis*, the average American touches their phone 2,617 times each day and spends two hours and thirty minutes staring at the small screen. Power users (aka most teens) touch their phones more than 5,000 times per day.[16] There is perhaps nothing more demanding of our attention and presence than smartphones.

I was once presenting at a seminar when a young guy asked me a direct question. I stopped and looked him in the eyes to answer. Mid-answer, he pulled out his phone and looked at it. I simply stopped talking and waited for him to finish. The whole room looked at him looking at his phone and me standing there waiting.

*He didn't notice.*

Eventually, we moved on with the seminar while he remained enraptured by his screen. That may sound ridiculous, but be honest: How often are your children, your friends, and even your wife waiting for you to look up from that little rectangle of glass?

## The TV Screen

One study revealed the typical Netflix user in the US watches 3.2 hours of Netflix a day.[17] Even if you are below that national average, the formative effect of being spoon-fed the narratives, values, and plotlines of the world begins to shape your mind and imagination. Shows today are designed to be addictive. Think about this for a moment: there are corporations spending billions of dollars trying to make sure *you stay glued to their content.* With so much competition and so many options, things like nudity, shock value, and intrigue are injected at precision levels to harvest our attention.

I am amazed how much knowledge people retain about their favorite shows. Complex character histories, multiseason plotlines, whole imaginary universes have taken root in our hearts. The same is true of sports: player profiles, statistics, teammates, histories—it is truly impressive. Men who can't remember where Paul's teachings on fatherhood are in the New Testament can give you the dynasty breakdown of the New York Yankees franchise history, era by era, player by player, across decades.

There is nothing inherently wrong with shows or sports, but when we know more about *Stranger Things* than the classes our kids are taking, the family dynamics of their closest friends, and the emerging complexities of their inner worlds, our priorities have been distorted.

## The Windshield

In some ways, one of the silver linings of COVID-19 was the ability to work from home. Though it can be stressful to have kids in the house while you're trying to work, and despite the emergence of things like Zoom fatigue, we collectively saved billions of hours of commuting time in 2020 through 2021. Many folks chose to leave urban areas and buy homes in locations they hadn't considered before, farther from the office than they would have considered pre-pandemic.

But as in-office work makes a comeback, many have longer commutes than they ever would have accepted before the pandemic, requiring earlier departures and later arrivals. According to the Census Bureau, the national average commute time in the United States had risen in 2022 to about 26.4 minutes one way, or nearly an hour round trip.[18]

Commutes aren't intrinsically bad. But building on the observations earlier in this chapter about the negative impact of the car on our ability to encounter one another, it's worth taking a close look at what your commute may be taking away from you. For too many of us, we take the best of our energy, put it in a car, and head into the world. At the end of the workday, we take what's left of our energy, get back in the car, and come home, with only scraps left over for the relationships and activities that should be our priorities.

# RESISTING A LIFE OF FRAGMENTATION

I'm not trying to be harsh here; I know life can be complicated. And a commute-free, screen-free life isn't realistic for most people. But we must understand how relationships work. We must nurture the love around us day by day, or it will die day by day. Even small amounts of notice and attention can be incredibly powerful for building relationships that can overcome the shadow of loneliness.

What can we do?

I'm glad you asked.

*Attention*, *participation*, and *place* are key. Here are some concrete strategies that can help you overcome the fragmenting, relationship-killing power that screens can exert over our lives.

## Attention

- **Put your phone to bed.** Leave your phone by the door when you come home. Have a place for your phone so you can get it when you need it, but don't treat it like an infant that needs to be attended to every time it cries. Put your phone "to bed" after a certain hour and don't pick it up until the next morning. Take advantage of the Focus or Digital Well-Being settings on your phones—they have changed my life. You can choose who you let through at what time, so you are always in touch with those who count on you but not at the mercy of those who don't.

- **Prioritize presence.** Reinvest the time you previously spent on your phone into simply being present and available—whether to friends or family. Some of my most definitive parenting and marriage moments have happened because I was paying attention, noticed what was going on, and leaned into my family members' lives.

## Participation

- *Live a better story.* Instead of watching fictional stories, work on living a better one. Get intentional about planning memorable hangs with friends. Become an expert on your kids' lives. Know the plotlines of your wife's heart. Track the key metrics around the call God has for you, not just the cultural realities over which you have little control.

- *Create "whimsy" moments.* Try creating one whimsy moment a day, a completely spontaneous and fun kind of moment, something that gets you in touch with a sense of wonder. This includes things like

  » jumping in the car and going for ice cream late at night,

  » getting on the subway and getting out at a random stop to explore the neighborhood, and

  » cooking a new dessert you have always wanted to make but never made the time to try.

## Place

- *Learn to love where you live.* Pay attention to the lives of your neighbors. Most of us will never change the world, but we can help heal our communities. We can be good news on our streets; we can open our doors and invite people in. We can listen to those who ache to be heard. We can contribute in small but tangible ways that reweave the shalom of God—wholeness and reconciliation—into local brokenness. Being present, being aware, being available, being content—this is how we love a place back to life. And when you begin to live in a particular place well, you'll be surprised at how your friendships begin to grow. They are enriched and made more robust.

## RELATIONSHIPS ARE INDISPENSABLE

Loneliness is not your destiny as a man. Beyond the emotional and physical benefits of friendship and community we've talked about in this chapter, you need to know that you were *created for community*. You were designed for friendship.

Think of Jesus for a second—he had a band of brothers and constantly reached out to sinners and tax collectors (the shamed of the day), fishermen (the blue-collar workers of the day), and even the religious elite, such as Nicodemus. And he became friends with those men by being in a place, by engaging in his everyday normal life, not just passing through it. By walking around together, paying attention to people, spending time eating together, and visiting one another's homes.

> You were *created for community.* You were designed for friendship.

Do you have space for those kinds of relationships? Are you

55

*making* space? After all, this book is about fighting shadows, and the shadow of loneliness is no exception. You will have to fight if you want to build deep, meaningful relationships in today's world.

We are discipled by community and in a community. Jesus called individual men, but he called them into a group. They became part of something greater and bigger. He made a team out of a bunch of individuals. He is still calling men together today—are you listening to the call?

If you're numbed by loneliness and wondering what happened to the deep, rich friendships you experienced earlier in life, ask yourself, *Did I try to coast on the fumes of those earlier seasons of community?* I thought I could ride for years the momentum of those close friendships I had in college. But I was wrong, and all of a sudden I was nearing my thirties and wondering where all my friends had gone. Instead of investing in relationships, I was serving a ruthless schedule, leaving little to no margin, and neglecting my friends all in the name of "focus" and "building something."

Thankfully, I had a wake-up call and realized I didn't want it to be that way for the rest of my life. I had to reverse the momentum. It took years and lots of coffees and fires and surf sessions. But guess what? Today, I can say that my friendships have never been richer—never been fuller. And it's because I've made it a priority and a core value. It's nonnegotiable, not just something I try to fit in "if I have time."

If Jesus' example of prioritizing friendship and real human connections while he was walking around on earth isn't enough, check this out: God himself is relational. We don't need to get into all the details of Trinitarian theology here. But let's just say that the very possibility of friendship—with one another and with God—all starts with the fact that God himself is a communion of persons. He is relational—Father, Son, and Spirit—eternally in a relationship of mutual love.

One of my favorite images is Andrei Rublev's famous icon known as *The Trinity*.[19] If you're not familiar with it, you should look it up online and google all the Russian eggs and subtle notes—it's absolutely packed with layers of meaning.

But I want to draw attention to one specific thing.

In the painting, the Father, Son, and Holy Spirit are gathered around a table. (Did you google it yet? You looking at it?) What is happening right there at the center? There's an empty space at the table. And the triune God is *inviting you to sit at that empty space*.

You are not alone. You have a seat with the Godhead. The Trinity is communal in nature. You are invited to sit at a table where there is already a community. You were created for community and are invited into community.

We are made in God's image, and we can only be faithful image bearers if we are in community.

Be present.

Participate in your own life.

Care about a place.

The kingdom of heaven will be found there—and the shadow of loneliness will have no power over your heart.

# THE SHADOW OF SHAME

*The Lie:* I need to do everything possible to prevent people from seeing my failures and weaknesses.
*The Truth:* God delights in you, even though you aren't perfect.

**There's a villain in the Spider-Man world—or** should we say, the Spider-Verse—called Venom. He looks similar to Spider-Man in figure, but instead of the familiar red-and-blue suit, he's dressed all in black, with downright monstrous features, including enormous fangs.

But Venom isn't really a person. Venom is a symbiote, which needs a host to grow within. When it finds a host, it eventually takes over that person. Several movies and cartoons have depicted Venom achieving this parasitic takeover of an unfortunate host: a black, gooey substance quickly engulfs the person, wrapping him or her up with octopus-like tentacles until the human is no more, and there is only Venom. Or rather, the person is overwhelmed and transformed by this parasite, which exploits the weaknesses of the host character and amplifies their worst traits, leading to all kinds of mayhem.

Venom's grotesque takeovers of human hosts provide an outstanding visual for illustrating and understanding shame.

That is what shame is.

That is what shame looks like.

That is what shame does.

It's a slimy shadow not only following us but trying to *swallow us whole*. It's a cloud that not only comes near to us but *becomes us*.

Now let's be clear: shame is not guilt.

Guilt is the sense that I have done something wrong.

Shame is the sense that there is fundamentally something *wrong with me*.

I (Jeff) have felt shame in all kinds of ways during my life, but when writing this book, I tried to think of the very first time I experienced shame. It took me a long time to dig it up, but then it hit me. Shame is what I felt but didn't have words for the first time I realized it wasn't normal for my dad not to be around. I realized he had made a conscious decision to not be there.

> Shame is the sense that there is fundamentally something *wrong with me*.

And this darkly toned question crept in—*Am I not good enough to be a son?*

That's when I first felt shame.

But it certainly wasn't the last.

Shame is what I felt when I got cut from the college baseball team—something I'd been training for and playing toward my whole life. *Am I not good enough to be on a team?* And it's what I felt when my first serious girlfriend broke up with me in college, when every part of me thought we'd get married. *Am I not good enough for her?*

Shame is the internalization of *There's something wrong with me. I'm gross, dirty, bad.* And the minute you give those thoughts power, shame settles over your heart and the poison begins to infect every facet of your being. Shame has destroyed countless men's lives.

We hide in the shadows of shame. We feel it deeply and begin to retreat in our hearts, minds, and emotions.

Pause for a moment and ask yourself, *Where is shame showing up in my life right now? Where is shame casting its shadow over my heart and mind?*

If you want to go "shame hunting," here are two helpful questions or smoke signals that will help you identify where shame is hiding in your life:

- What's the place you are scared to be bold or creative? Shame almost always holds us back from our destiny and purpose.
- What's an area where you spend a lot of time and energy hiding the real you? Shame convinces us our survival depends on hiding imperfections, weaknesses, and embarrassing parts of ourselves.

Is shame casting its long shadow over your life? You're not alone. We will probably remind you that you're not alone in just about every chapter of this book—but it bears repeating. Every shadow we name and battle in these pages is widespread. We picked these particular shadows after countless conversations and moments with men in the trenches. Sometimes just naming the reality that you're not alone is an important step toward the light.

Shame sends you into hiding. It's a form of slavery, and it will do everything in its power to keep you from living out God's call on your life.

Let's do battle.

## THE PRIMAL NATURE OF SHAME

Curt Thompson, one of the foremost experts on shame today, noted that you can't just think your way out of shame. Now, some proponents of cognitive behavioral therapy (CBT) say or imply that you can. CBT is a very helpful framework for behavior change based on thinking new thoughts to kill the old thoughts. But I don't think CBT goes far enough when it comes to shame.

That's because shame is primal. It has been embedded in our souls ever since the garden of Eden.

Thompson said the reason trying to think your way out of shame never works is because there are three layers *before* you get to the "think better" stage. Shame forms in a particular order.

First, it's *felt*.
Then *sensed*.
Then *imaged*.
And, finally, it is *thought*.

Of course, this sequence happens in a flash. But that buildup from *feeling* to *thinking* is significant. A primal, dark, negative emotion strikes you first. You simply feel it. Then it goes physiological—you sense it. Then you picture it. Then, and only then, does it take up residence in your mind as a conscious thought.

This is important because a lot of us assume that we start the battle over shame at the moment we first think about it. But that's already way far down the road. We need to look for ways to get to the root of the issue, to sense and image anti-shame.

Note that shame isn't sin per se, though it is closely associated with sinful impulses and reactions. Shame starts as an emotional, physical, and mental reaction to feeling exposed, vulnerable, and scrutinized. Any time we see that we have failed, made a mistake, or sinned, there's a powerful impulse to hide. We don't want to see our failure or inadequacy. And we *certainly* don't want other people to see it. Under the massive pressure of shame, our natural tendency is to hide, deflect, distract—anything to escape the feeling that we're unworthy, ugly, or bad.

Let's take a closer look at what's going on with shame—why it hits us the way it does, and why it casts such a long shadow over men's hearts.

## HOW SHAME WORKS

Shame causes chaos. Shame is, at its heart, a spirit of *disintegration*. It rips things apart that were meant to be unified. And shame's impact on us is incredibly destructive. It introduces a series of cracks or rifts—it separates us from our own hearts, from other people, and worst of all from God. It strips us of our ability to create beauty and do good.

Why? Because shame is a corrosive force against the creative order. It's anti-creation.

This is an important point, so stay with me for a second.

When God spun creation into existence, he began unleashing his beauty and goodness into the world—and he does that especially through humans, his agents and image bearers. But shame is primarily an evil force used by the Enemy to attack and wound God's creation. It's that slime or poison—like the Venom symbiote—that engulfs and corrodes everything it touches. Shame is an antithetical force. It attempts to reverse creation's momentum, pulling things away from order and back into chaos. It doesn't have the ability to create new life or beauty. It is parasitic, anti-life, and anti-beauty.

Notice that shame entered the biblical story only when humans stepped outside God's design for us as image bearers. And significantly, God never put shame on humans. In fact, he mercifully *covered* their shame, sacrificing animals and clothing Adam and Eve in those animals' skins. What a picture of Jesus and his redemptive work to come. But Satan used shame to hurt Adam and Eve and push them deeper into hiding, further into darkness. It is exclusively a tactical weapon of the Enemy—I'd even argue it's his *paramount* weapon.

We are still fighting the same battle. We are being pushed further and further into the shadows under the burden of shame, whether in response to our failures, our weaknesses, or our inability to live up to a standard we have in our heads.

### The Shame Spiral

Tragically, what keeps most men stuck in shame is the misguided belief that we can get out of shame by ourselves. But it doesn't work like that. Curt Thompson said, "Shame always requires outside help for healing."[1]

That reality is a big part of why shame is such a destructive force for men. If we struggle asking help for directions, how hard do you think it'll be to share the darkest recesses of our hearts?

Seeking outside help for our shame is not easy, but it is necessary for us to flourish as men.

In other words, to be eradicated, shame requires light and exposure, and that only happens through relationship and presence—the very thing shame makes us want to run from. No wonder shame is so difficult to overcome. It hits us hardest in the very place that holds the possibility of healing. That's the power of the cycle of shame. Once the cycle reaches the point where you start having the conscious thought that you are not good enough, shame doubles back to reinforce your feelings and sense of inadequacy and failure. What a tragically effective strategy for the Enemy. But the first step to beating an enemy is being aware of his schemes.

Many of us men are not very good at making that connection from feeling and sensing to forming thoughts. But as long as we continue to battle shame by trying to *think* our way out of it, we will fail miserably. It's just not possible. Fighting shame by trying to think harder is like trying to put out a fire in your house by thinking harder. Thinking just isn't the right tool for the job.

> **Seeking outside help for our shame is not easy, but it is necessary for us to flourish as men.**

Curt Thompson gave a great example of a man named Matt who was successful in business many times over, but his anxiety and worry were beginning to become crippling. Matt tried therapy and reciting Scripture to replace his harmful thoughts with helpful thoughts, but it wasn't working. Thompson went on to explain:

> Further exploration revealed that under all of this was a deep *sense* that he simply did not have what it took to be effective, a sensation that was not reducible to a statement but rather something that seemed to have been woven into his DNA. Although we often try to get our minds around shame by using language (which is not unimportant), its essence precedes language; we therefore often have difficulty regulating it by using words. Telling ourselves we shouldn't be ashamed often only reinforces it.[2]

And so back to the picture of shame as anti-creation. You need to recognize shame as a force. It's a force that takes you backward when God is trying to take you forward. It's a force that disintegrates when God is trying to integrate. C. S. Lewis's imagery in *The Great Divorce* is key. If you haven't read this book, I recommend you get a copy—it's one of my personal favorites.[3]

In that book, Lewis describes the citizens of heaven as weighty, which Lewis equated with the idea of glory. Glory has a weight of power. Those in heaven have been made more and more into God's image not by hiding but by facing toward him in faith. Slowly over time they have become weightier, more substantial, more real, more *glorious*.

But the citizens in hell? They live in pure isolation. The nearest neighbor lives thousands of miles away from the other. And they are ghostly—airy, thin, almost translucent. Why? Because that's exactly what anti-creation does. It rips and steals and breaks the glory out of us. The seed of glory—the image of God in us—is what makes us human, but by choosing a life of disobedience and "hiding" on earth, humans become shadows of their former selves.

In Lewis's story, the citizens of hell get bussed to heaven one day, and when they arrive, they can't even walk on the grass in heaven without serious pain. Even grass in heaven is more glorious than they are, and it pierces their feet like sharp spikes.

If we let shame win, our true self, the image of God in us being formed into Jesus' likeness, slowly begins to corrode—to dissipate, to crumble.

But if we defiantly stay in the light? Glory.

## HOW TO FEED YOUR SHAME

We mentioned earlier that the impulse to hide is one of the hallmarks of shame. Adam and Eve were naked and unashamed before the fall, but when they chose disobedience and fractured the cosmos, what was the first thing they did?

*Hide.*

Many of us don't hide when we encounter feelings of shame. But we hide parts of ourselves—often in the name of masculinity. We've been taught to believe we need to be tough and never show weakness. We fear that showing where we have been hurt will make us appear weak. Vulnerability about our failures and weaknesses feels like death for many men. And to some degree, it is. Vulnerability is the death of pride and isolation. It is loudly admitting and showing you cannot solve your own problems.

My wife, Alyssa, would say to this day some of the more intimate and connected moments she's ever felt in our marriage were when I shared something deeply vulnerable I was wrestling with. Think how strange and ironic that is. The lie shame tells us is that if we're vulnerable, the world will fall apart. In fact, the opposite is true: moments of sharing are when you tend to find mending and healing.

Where does that leave us? How can we fight the shadow of shame when it seems like we're wired for it—not only as humans, but especially as men who have been trained to disavow our weakness and refuse to recognize our vulnerability?

## HOW TO EAT YOUR SHADOW

I (Jeff) still remember my most recent major encounter with shame and the power of vulnerability.

It required me to dig seriously into *Why am I feeling this so strongly?* and *Why is this shaking me in such a big way?*

I think most men assume shame only (or mostly) shows up as sexual shame. And, of course, that's a significant part of many men's journeys. We'll chat about that in the upcoming chapter on the shadow of lust. But this instance of shame related to failure and control. It all began when I was still in my twenties and had made a few partnerships with folks around some business ideas.

One of these was a partner to whom I gave a considerable amount of ownership over a key area of my career. Let's call this guy Joe. I saw Joe's ability to further people's efforts and grow their work into something meaningful, so when he said he could help I hopped in, no questions asked.

I remember a mentor warning me at the time, "Jeff, be careful to make sure any business partner you take on has the same values as you. Because when any disagreements come around, someone's values usually drive them."

I wasn't careful to make sure.

I was excited. I was young. I thought I knew what I was doing.

And to be honest, things did grow. In fact, things went very, very well—for years. And I'm thankful to him for all of that.

But then Joe started making some life decisions I felt were unwise—even dangerous and harmful to himself and to others. I became concerned that, because of our association, his actions could jeopardize my integrity and character. And I had worked *so* hard to keep my work firmly rooted in integrity.

Alyssa and I began to wrestle with what to do. One morning, Alyssa woke up and said, "I just had a super vivid dream. It was a picture of where Joe is going and it's not good, and I'm concerned he's taking us there with him. You need to email Joe right now and tell him we are parting ways, whatever the consequences."

Pro tip: if you have a Spirit-led wife who knows the Lord intimately, listen to her immediately. I can probably count on one hand all the moments Alyssa has spoken a "God told me directly" moment in our marriage, so I knew it was serious. Also, it was one of those rare moments where I felt that *not* listening to

Alyssa's words would be disobedience to God, not just a marriage disagreement with my spouse. I felt that in my spirit.

I emailed Joe that very moment. My email was gracious and gentle. I made sure he knew I wished him the best, and I asked him to work with us to find the easiest way to untangle our business relationship.

Now, for additional context, when you're in a business relationship with someone, *everything* gets tangled up—finances, websites, relationships. And while I don't want to share all the details, I'll just say that it takes the cooperation of all parties to unravel this kind of business relationship peacefully.

From Joe's response, it soon became clear to me that we were in for a battle. And sure enough, I soon found myself in one of the most difficult, embarrassing, and damaging conflicts I'd ever been in. The kind of conflict where I began to fear that everything Joe and I had built together would come crashing down, taking my reputation with it.

And let me tell you, something broke in me. I have not felt shame that deeply in my entire life. And the most frustrating part is I didn't quite know why. It was as if something primal got touched, something that I didn't yet have the skill set to dig deep enough to understand.

The entire thing dragged out for months and months. I experienced visceral reactions in my body. I couldn't sleep. I couldn't eat. It felt emotionally like the worst breakup plus the biggest financial fiasco.

Pure shame.

My reaction caught me by surprise, though. Why was this affecting me so deeply? And why *shame* of all things?

THE SHADOW OF SHAME

It took me a while to dig in and figure out what was going on—counseling, mentors, my wife, journaling, Scripture reading.

Eventually, it started to become clear. I realized my deep sense of shame over this imploded business partnership was because I had built my entire life around a desire never to get screwed over.

Never be gullible.
Never get played.
Always be in control.

In my shame, I despised my helplessness. I wanted to run from that feeling at all costs.

The reason for this? Growing up in a single-parent household, I'd felt helpless my entire childhood. My dad wasn't around much, but when he was, he was extremely unstable emotionally, which is scary for a kid. My mom was amazing, but she struggled with mental illness. She couldn't hold a steady job, so we spent a lot of time in government housing, relying on food stamps, and moving around here and there.

I learned about survival early on. I believed I was on my own. And I learned very quickly a lesson that proved to be a counterfeit: that the best way to succeed in life was to have *control*. I believed if I had the power and control, no one could screw me over.

As I started unpacking the sources of the shame I felt about how everything went down with Joe, I realized one of the motivating impulses of my life was *never to be or feel helpless again*. And there I was, twenty-seven years old, feeling helpless, staring down the possibility of losing everything I'd worked for my entire adult life.

I had zero control.

I felt *so stupid*.

And I couldn't do anything about it.

It ended up being a sort of baptism by fire. And weirdly, I'm glad it happened because it was one of the most life-shaping events I've ever experienced. It made me face my shame—and work on it.

And let me be clear—when I say "work on it," I mean a slow, arduous process of mainly self-discovery illuminated by God's voice over the deepest and darkest parts of my heart. It was a multiyear process to discover what I just wrote about the last few pages. This is what Robert Bly called "eating our shadow."

"Eating our shadow is a very slow process. It doesn't happen once, but hundreds of times," wrote Bly.[4]

My shadow of shame was the shame of my childhood—the shame of being helpless and having zero agency, the shadow of embarrassment over my life circumstances, the shame of my dad's not being around or in the home or teaching me a single thing.

And that shadow followed me, as shadows naturally do.

Just because a shadow is quiet doesn't mean it can't engulf you in darkness. In fact, just like my shadow of shame in this story, it will stick around and keep growing *until you face it and deal with it*.

And while God can do miraculous works of healing in a flash—and sometimes he does—I've found more often than not that flash moment is embedded in a longer season of just doing the very, very, very hard work of facing your demons and working through them with his help.

You have to face it. And you have to eat it.

When I think of eating your shadow, I think of Willie Sutton. He was nicknamed the "Babe Ruth of bank robbers" due to his daring robberies for which he relied on his charm, wit, and clever disguises. He also could have been called the Babe Ruth of prison escapes—he managed to escape from three different prisons. He may seem like an unusual choice for an object lesson in this chapter about shame, but bear with me.

In 1934, Sutton was sentenced to several decades in prison for his crimes. And the prison wasn't a nice one. Eastern State Penitentiary's mission statement included the line, "a prison designed to create genuine regret and penitence in the criminal's heart."[5]

After several failed attempts, Sutton partnered up with eleven other inmates and hatched an escape plan. Relying on the construction knowledge of fellow inmate Clarence "Kliney" Klinedinst, they drew up plans for an escape tunnel. Starting in cell sixty-eight, they created an opening in the wall, dug straight down about twelve feet, and then about a hundred feet horizontally, just beyond the limits of the prison wall.

There were about a dozen of them. And after some preliminary planning, they started digging. The plan was to dig a tunnel hundreds of feet underground.

Their primary tools for this massive undertaking? Spoons.

It took nearly two years to complete, with a dozen men working in thirty-minute shifts. They disguised the tunnel opening in cell sixty-eight with a panel that Kliney prepared to match the prison's plaster walls—a simple but effective method that withstood multiple inspections over the many months it took them to complete the project.

Sutton and his crew removed the dirt little by little by placing spoonfuls in their pockets and dispersing it in the prison yard throughout the day. The tunnel had scaffolding and lighting. It was even ventilated. When they encountered a sewage pipe halfway through, they figured out a way to reroute the prison sewer system.

The scale of the undertaking, given the limited tools and resources available to them, was unbelievable. *They dug out of prison with a spoon.*

Now, Sutton isn't a great role model—though there's something charming about his commitment never to use violence, his reputation for extreme politeness, and the sheer daring of both his robberies and his escapes. I'm just amazed at the story of this escape and the sheer dedication. And I can't think of a better illustration of what it takes to eat the shadow of shame. It's a huge task, and it can only be accomplished one spoonful at a time.

You will never run out of opportunities for shame to overshadow your heart. We're finite, sinful people. We're going to fail. We're going to make mistakes. We're going to run up against the limits of our strength. Our weaknesses will show up at the very moment people are watching us. And when those things happen, we have a choice.

And it's very important we make the right choice.

We can try to hide our failures behind bragging about our accomplishments, or disguise our weaknesses by acting tough, or deflect attention to our vulnerability through aggression.

Or we can take the route of humble honesty, pick up that spoon, and start excavating the depths of our weaknesses and failures. The reality is that it takes a lot more strength to eat that shadow, day after day, than it does to hide behind a mask of invulnerability. Hiding is easy. It destroys us in the end, but it's easy in the moment.

But living in the light? Fighting the shadows? That's where life is.

## TWO TEMPTATIONS, ONE SOLUTION

When shame seeps into the cracks in your heart, you as a man will likely be tempted by a couple of false solutions.

The first is the temptation of religion.

You'll be tempted to clean yourself up by treating your shame like a debt you can repay via religious means—sacrifice, penance, going to church that Sunday, giving to the poor . . . you get the idea. These are all good things, by the way! But they do nothing for your shame. Trying to heal your shame with religion is like trying to fight a forest fire with a kid's water squirt gun. You won't put out a single flame.

The second temptation is distraction.

Where the temptation of religion is to think you can self-clean your shame, distraction invites you to numb your feelings of shame.

Let's be honest with ourselves. Shame can get very loud. *It feels like real pain.*

And what do we do with pain?

We medicate.

When it comes to shame, we are so easily tempted to try to

make it go away by feeling something else stronger. That something else could be sex, whether illicit sex or with our spouse. It could be money, whether gambling or a wise business investment. It could be food, whether an unhealthy addiction to food or just food in general.

Whether the distraction is fundamentally bad or something that is fine, if we are using it to drown and medicate the shame, it's going to cause harm. And even if your efforts lead to temporary relief, they're not going to solve your shame problem.

You can't fix your shame with religion or bury it with distraction. There's only one real solution—an *invitation*—an invitation from God himself.

He invites us not to religiously modify our shame or medicate our shame. He offers to *heal our shame*. And for that to happen, we need to drag our shame into God's presence, where he speaks not just *about* us but *to* us, telling us the truth about who we are and how he sees us.

## GOD DELIGHTS IN YOU

Here's a wild truth I suspect most men don't realize. God isn't ashamed of you. He isn't disappointed in you. He delights in your presence.

Make sure you read that again. I said he delights in *your* presence. I know it's already a leap for men in the shadows to believe God wants them in *his* presence. But taking it a step further, God wants to be in *your* presence. He delights in relational closeness with you, and he's moving toward you. Like a father hopping down on the floor to play blocks with a child, God enjoys coming down to be with you on your level.

*But you need to invite him.*

And when you do take that difficult first step into God's presence and allow yourself not just to *believe the idea* but to *experience the reality* of God's delight in you, shame dissipates so fast. Think back to Curt Thompson's observations about how shame forms and the impossibility of thinking your way out of shame. It starts as a feeling, then becomes something you sense and image, and only then does it become a conscious thought. Here, in the presence of the God who delights in you, is where you break that shame cycle, where you interrupt the spiral. Instead of just telling yourself to think about the idea that God delights in you, you need to feel it, sense it, image it. His delight needs to seep into your soul.

In practical terms, you need to come to God with the parts you hate most about yourself, not just the parts you love—the struggles you wish you didn't have, the parts of your story and life and mind you wish weren't there.

When you bring those things into his presence, with no facade of perfection, and lay them down at his feet, all you will find is love.

# THE SHADOW OF LUST

*The Lie:* I am a slave to my sexual desire.

*The Truth:* Faithfulness is a key to my formation.

*Because I longed for eternal life, I went to bed with harlots and drank for nights on end.*

**—ALBERT CAMUS**

*There is no dignity when the human dimension is eliminated from the person. In short, the problem with pornography is not that it shows too much of the person, but that it shows far too little.*

**—POPE JOHN PAUL II**

**I (Jon) am eight years old and standing in the** bathroom of a local swimming center in Perth, Western Australia. Laid out before me are dozens of images of naked women and I cannot turn my eyes away.

A stranger has strewn pornography across the bathroom for all to see. A warm feeling of both attraction and guilt is rushing over my body, and I have no control over this. I have heard about sex before, but it was always something at a distance, something adult, something other—curious, but inaccessible.

I thought I would simply wait to grow up and figure things out as they came along. But this changes things. This feeling, this longing, this woman with a welcoming smile with her naked body and hollow eyes. I quickly fold the pages up and think about how I can smuggle these back to my room for further examination.

This is the first time in my life I have seen pornography. I did not seek this out. I did not ask for the shadow to fall on the innocence of my life. Yet I will never unsee these images. Something has been awakened. Where were you when the shadow of lust first fell over your life?

. . .

I am fourteen years old and standing in front of a bed covered with *Penthouse* magazines. I am at my friend's house after school, one of my only friends I have worked hard to make, and I don't have the relational capital to say no to the magazines. A forbidden visual feast, my friend tells me to take a look and take my time; his dad won't be home for hours.

My conscience still works, but the temptation is too much, so I pick up a magazine and begin to look. These images are more explicit somehow. The women seem confident and defiant. After a few minutes I simply say "cool" enough times that he gathers them up and puts them under his father's side of the bed. But the images won't simply go back on the pages and hide in the dark. They are in my mind, and I do not know how to get them out. This is the second time in my life I have seen pornography.

. . .

I am eighteen years old and now a follower of Jesus. I am holding a *Playboy* magazine. Every part of my body is awakened and focused. I look at these images for several minutes and then close the magazine and put it back on the coffee table.

I am at the house of a friend who is not a Christian, and I am trying to build a relationship with him so I can share the gospel. I did not anticipate he would be sharing his porn. And now I feel a deep sense of guilt because this is something I have chosen, something I could not resist. In the grand scope of my life, this will not seem like a massive thing—a magazine, a few moments, a friend's house. But the first violation of the renewed conscience is the first step of a journey into habitual sin. The shadow of lust will not be retreating behind the sun.

As hard as it may seem to those of you who grew up with laptops and cell phones, that was the extent of all the pornography I saw growing up. Porn was something you couldn't get your hands on easily. It involved shady stores and sketchy men coming in and out with secrecy and shame. There was no "online" anything, no "hubs" to doomscroll your way through.

Just a few scattered moments, but neurological pathways were formed. There was temptation where I grew up, girls and parties and beer and drugs. But porn? Unless your older brother had a stash or a friend's dad was careless, naked women existed in the imagination or awkward coming-of-age moments. Porn wasn't normal, it wasn't accessible, and it certainly wasn't culturally acceptable.

## THE PORNIFICATION OF EVERYTHING

Fast-forward a couple of decades and everything has changed. Sex has come out of the bedroom into every part of our lives. It's estimated that 81 percent of major motion pictures and 82 percent of mainstream TV programs contain sexual content.

Compare my experiences growing up to what is normalized in high schools today. *The New York Times* ran an article on how some schools even teach "Porn Literacy":

> For around two hours each week, for five weeks, the students—sophomores, juniors, and seniors—take part in Porn Literacy, which aims to make them savvier, more critical consumers of porn by examining how gender, sexuality, aggression, consent, race, queer sex, relationships, and body images are portrayed (or, in the case of consent, not portrayed) in porn.[1]

The course has a more official title, The Truth About Pornography: A Pornography Literacy Curriculum for High School Students Designed to Reduce Sexual and Dating Violence.[2]

But you get the idea.

The goal isn't to stop teens from watching porn but to help them become more thoughtful consumers of porn.

I'm not sure what your first exposure to sex was or the specifics of how it has shaped you since, but I know lust is one of the dominant shadows falling across the hearts of men today. When we talk with Christian men, far too often we find there is so much shame and guilt around their sexuality. Men seem to instinctively know sex is something sacred, a gift from God, yet they are also hyperaware that sex is a gift that is prone to distortion and abuse.

In fact, when a young man wants to talk these days about something he is struggling with, it's almost a given that it's going to be sex. The sexual revolution has destroyed traditional values about sex, marriage, and family. Any sense of sanctity, chastity, or innocence is gone. Nietzsche made the claim that God was dead and that we had killed him. Who could have known the weapon would feel so good? Where God was once at the center of cultural life, we now worship at the altar of sex.

## PROBLEMATIC REACTIONS TO THESE CULTURAL CHANGES

Because of the potency of sex, and Scripture's teaching on it, the changes in sexuality have not gone unchallenged. I will expand on this later in this chapter. But to say what seems obvious in our lived experience, there is so much confusion, temptation, abuse, and pain that seems to be impacting our lives.

Making love has been changed into waging war; sex has been weaponized against us all. Many of us feel like casualties in this war. There have been two main reactions to the battle for human sexuality, and these two reactions have caused a cycle of shame and lust that almost all of us have felt in our bones.

### Reaction #1: Repression

The first response has been to shut down our sexual desire.

The church has been the main proponent for this response to sex. Sex has been viewed as a force so dominant that it must be shut down. And the Bible is filled with examples of sexual desire gone wrong. Who can forget Judah's hypocrisy (Genesis 38), David's lust (2 Samuel 11–12), Solomon's concubines (1 Kings 11), or the Corinthian church's immorality (1 Corinthians 5)?

And you probably have your own stories of lust you felt

powerless to control. Sex has started wars, soiled saints, and shut down kingdoms. "Sex must be repressed" is the rallying cry for some in the church who focus primarily on the ways sex has been a destructive force.

And then there's also purity culture.

Purity culture is a movement in churches and youth groups to get young people to commit to sexual abstinence before marriage. Purity culture gained traction especially in the 1990s. High schoolers were given purity rings and purity talks, warnings were issued about the dangers of lust and promiscuity, and purity was categorized as a divine commodity.

As the joke went at the time, "Sex is such a dirty and dangerous thing; make sure you save it for the person you love."

Promises were made—such great promises. If you waited till you were married, bliss would be your reward. You would have kids, be blessed, and enjoy the kind of sex that pagans only dreamed about. But then a generation of kids grew up, got married, and realized the amazing sex they'd been promised was embodied in relational complexities they were not prepared for.

Rather than a solution, purity culture became an idolized struggle that caused unrealistic expectations, unsustainable pressure, and deep disappointment. True love waited, but for what? The evangelical idol of marriage failed its promises for far too many.

During the process, damage was done as well. Purity got weaponized against women, while guys got away with "struggling." Purity became the only measure of a woman's worth. Many young women felt worthless and shamed when these standards were broken, and many young men became both self-righteous and self-loathing at the same time. There was a false assumption about how holiness worked. It went something like this:

MORAL STANDARDS + WILLPOWER = HOLINESS

I believe it's important to teach young people about the potency and power of sex. I believe teenagers need grace-filled conversations in a world of moral chaos. I believe sex before marriage is wrong.

But much of what was taught by purity culture—and is still being taught in many churches today—created cycles of guilt and shame and hopelessness that still haunt so many. And over time it has become clear that this framework was a formula not for holiness but for embarrassment and disgrace.

As Philip Yancey has pointed out,

I know of no greater failure among Christians than in presenting a persuasive point of view on sexuality. Outside the church, people think of God as the great spoilsport of human sexuality, not its inventor. In a sex-saturated society, even true believers find it hard to accept that traditional Christian morality offers the fullest, most satisfying life. The pope utters pronouncements, denominations issue position papers, and many Christians ignore them and follow the lead of the rest of society. Surveys reveal little difference between church attenders and nonattenders in the rates of premarital intercourse and cohabitation. Surveys also show that millions of people have left the church in disgust over its hypocrisy about sex, especially when priests and ministers fail to practice what they preach.[3]

Here is the truth. The fear and repression formula ends up looking like this:

$$\text{Moral Standards} + \text{Willpower} =$$
$$\text{Failure, Guilt, and Shame}$$

I have met with so many men over the years who were trapped in a cycle of sexual failure, men reaching toward purity but without the power to maintain it. The cycle goes like this:

*Try harder:* Fail. Quit. Shame.
*Try harder:* Fail. Quit. Guilt.
*Try again:* Fail. Quit. Sadness.

Seem familiar?

The problem with the repression view is that *it doesn't take sex seriously enough.*

It highlights the dangers of sex without revealing the purpose of sex. It removes sex from its relational setting and commodifies it within a kind of moral economy. In fact, Jerome, the famous translator of the Latin Vulgate, even came up with a point system for women based on their sexual purity, which Philip Yancey summarized as "a hundred for virgins, sixty for widows, and thirty for married women, ranking marriage just above fornication."[4]

Repressing sexual desire and abstaining for religious reasons became an obsession of the church:

Church authorities issued edicts forbidding sex on Thursdays, the day of Christ's arrest; on Fridays, the day of his death;

on Saturdays, in honor of the blessed Virgin; and on Sundays in honor of the departed saints. Wednesdays sometimes made the list too, as did the forty-day fast periods before Easter, Christmas, and Pentecost, and also feast days and days of the apostles, as well as the days of female impurity. The list escalated until . . . only forty-four days a year remained available for marital sex.[5]

What a tragedy that God is seen as the great spoiler of sexuality, not its inventor. This is a tragic misunderstanding of his heart and plan.

### Reaction #2: Unrestrained Indulgence

The second reaction has been to release any control over your desires.

This response is about removing the stigma around all sexual practices so there is nothing to be sorry for. The world has often looked at the church's teaching on sex and seen it as restrictive and repressive. In response it launched a quest to take back sex for itself—enter the *sexual revolution*. The word choice is fitting. A revolution seeks to overthrow a regime and replace it with another. Let's take a closer look at the sexual revolution and how it has deformed our relationship with sex.

## HOW DID WE GET HERE?

According to Mary Eberstadt, the sexual revolution was "the destigmatization and demystification of nonmarital sex and the reduction of sexual relations in general to a kind of hygienic recreation in which anything goes so long as those involved are consenting adults."[6]

Sexual recreation among consenting adults—this is modern secular life. And this revolution has been widely televised. In this view, sex is seen as simply a natural appetite.

If you are thirsty, you drink water.

If you are hungry, you eat steak.

If you are aroused, you hook up with someone or masturbate to porn.

Releasing your sexual desire comes with its own formula. It's almost become a mantra of our world today:

$$\text{DESIRE} + \text{CONSENT} = \text{FREEDOM}$$

You are told you must be sex positive; you need to be free; people need space to become who they truly are. We need to remove the stigmatizing labels and categories that hold us back— sex without shame, sex without consequence, sex with whoever, however you want.

For many men, this new sexual vision has been intoxicating. Before we even leave our beds in the morning, we can see more porn than a previous generation would have seen in a lifetime.

We can sleep with more women in college than other generations thought possible. But strangely, despite the societal access of what amounts to a permanent spring break, we don't seem to be much happier. We may not be repressing sex, but we don't seem more satisfied either. That's because you can't reduce sex to a mere commodity, an economy of pleasurable exchange.

Ronald Rolheiser observed the following:

For a Christian, sex is something sacred. Hence it can never be simply a casual, unimportant, neutral thing. If its proper nature is respected, it builds the soul as a sacrament, and brings God's physical touch to us. Conversely, though, if its proper nature is not respected, it becomes a perverse thing that works at disintegrating the soul.[7]

The truth is our culture's version of freedom doesn't work. In reality,

## DESIRE + CONSENT = DISILLUSIONMENT AND DEFORMATION

The world has forgotten something. Sex isn't just about fulfillment; it's about formation. Sex is one of the most potent forces that shapes our lives. And the way we have been using sex has deeply deformed us as men.

First Corinthians 6:18 says, "All other sins a person commits are outside the body, but whoever sins sexually, sins against their own body." We almost always think of sexual sin as something we do with others or something we do to others. In some sense this is correct. Sexual abuse and assault weave power and sexuality into a heartbreaking abuse of power. But when we sin sexually, we are also sinning against ourselves. We don't just do abusive things; we become abusive men. We don't just watch misogynistic porn; we develop a misogynistic mindset.

The radical pursuit of sex has made us the wrong kind of men.

## A Deformed View of Women

Women are often seen as commodities for male consumption. Pornography, often filmed from the perspective of the male gaze, emphasizes male power while stripping women of their personhood and reducing them to objects of pleasure. In a recent survey of sixteen- to eighteen-year-old Americans, "many of the young women said they were pressured to play out the 'scripts' their male partners had learned from porn. They felt badgered into having sex in uncomfortable positions, faking sexual responses, and consenting to unpleasant or painful acts."[8]

The American Psychological Association noted that "the saturation of sexualized images of females is leading to body hatred, eating disorders, low self-esteem, depression."[9] Put all that into the stories of Christian men, and it complicates the church's ability to disciple men and build healthy and safe environments for women.

## Deformed Sexual Appetites

Porn has become increasingly violent. Porn addiction affects the brain in such a way that the same kinds of images no longer give a dopamine hit. So sex gets more and more violent, and the brain fires and wires sex and violence together.

We are normalizing domestic violence through our sexual fantasies without even knowing it. "Porn sites are the window to the modern soul; they're glimpses into the twisted minds of a faceless society," said Chuck Klosterman. "All the deviancy Freud tried to deduce through decades of analysis is now completely exposed. When Carl Jung introduced the concept of the 'collective unconscious,' he was trying to explain why all humans are inherently scared of things like darkness and vampires—but porn is the collective consciousness. It's where we all see the things people would never admit to wanting."[10]

And what we want has become evil. I can't even list the top-searched categories of online porn here.

## A Deformed Commitment

The rise of hook-up culture and dating apps has removed the normal, slow process of relationship building, friendship, and love.

They have removed the friction and tension, replacing it with sex with strangers. I asked a woman in New York, a leader I deeply respect, what impact dating apps have had on the relational dynamics of meeting men and building commitment. I have never forgotten her reply. "Dating apps are like Amazon Prime to deliver you hot people."[11]

More and more people don't bother with marriage even if they stay together. Living together unmarried, once a source of scandal, is considered normal. But Jonathan Grant pointed out that attempting to enjoy the benefits of commitment without making a commitment has not worked out so well:

- Only 1 in 5 cohabiting relationships ends in marriage.
- Cohabiting significantly increases the likelihood of divorce.
- Women who cohabit multiple times before marrying divorce more than twice as frequently as those who live only with their future husband.
- Serial monogamy—that is, a string of consecutive sexual relationships—hinders eventual marital satisfaction, while sexual experience before marriage is a good indicator for an increased likelihood of infidelity within marriage.

## A Deformed Sense of Self

Sex with strangers or masturbating to porn will not lead to fulfillment for men seeking to live the way of Jesus. Both cause us to collapse within ourselves. Instead of being drawn out into the real world where much is required of us, we collapse inward where nothing but our pleasure matters. C. S. Lewis wrote about the dangers of masturbation from that angle—not because of its moral dynamic per say, but because of how it forms our sexual desires:

> For me the real evil of masturbation would be that it takes an appetite which, in lawful use, leads the individual out of himself to complete (and correct) his own personality in that of another (and finally in children and even grandchildren) and turns it back: sends the man back into the prison of himself, there to keep a harem of imaginary brides. And this harem, once admitted, works against his ever getting out and really uniting with a real woman. For the harem is always accessible, always subservient, calls for no sacrifices or adjustments, and can be endowed with erotic and psychological attractions which no real woman can rival. Among these shadowy brides he is always adored, always the perfect lover: no demand is made on his unselfishness, no mortification is ever imposed on his vanity. In the end, they become merely the medium through which he increasingly adores himself.[12]

Men with imaginary harems, men living in the prison of themselves, men admiring themselves in a sexual illusion—this is the legacy of the sexual revolution.

The shadow of sexualization has fallen on an entire generation of men. God created Eve as a complement for man, not as a substitute for God. But the Enemy's plan is to place sex in front of God in such a way that God disappears. The shadow of sexualization eclipses God and casts a shadow over our hearts. All that is left in our view of life is sex, power, pleasure, and women.

God is blocked out of our conscious reality. Sex has become salvation. As Rolheiser noted, "Our age has turned sex into a soteriology, a doctrine of salvation. In other words, sex isn't perceived as a means toward heaven; it is identified with heaven itself. It's what we're supposed to be living for."[13] All false gospels enslave and destroy. The gospel of sex is no exception. Satan appears as an angel of light. He has no problem showing up as an angel of love. God created Eve as an equal because it wasn't good for man to be alone. The Enemy turned her into an idol, and she has been sexualized and stigmatized ever since. And modern men seem more alone than ever.

## SEXUAL FORMATION AND THE WAY OF JESUS

The way of Jesus is not about repression or indulgence; it's about the redirection and transformation of our desires.

This is a key distinction.

Sexuality should be about routing our longings as men into that which will deeply satisfy, transforming us into the men we ache to be.

God doesn't want us to repress our sexuality; he wants to connect it.

97

God doesn't want us to release our sexuality; he wants to
   protect it.
God doesn't want to remove our sexuality; he wants to
   redirect it.

Sex is not just about morality, pleasure, power, or pain. It is a
sign that points beyond itself. God wants to use our sexuality as
a tool of spiritual formation to make us more like Christ. As men
we need to recategorize our thinking about
sex. The idea of sexual
formation changes the
questions we ask about
our sexuality.

> **Sexuality should be about routing our longings as men into that which will deeply satisfy, transforming us into the men we ache to be.**

Rather than asking,
Is what I am doing sinful? or Is what I am doing allowed? we
need to ask:

- *Who am I becoming by what I am doing?*
- *Who am I becoming by what I am doing with my sexuality?*

These are the kinds of questions Paul posed to the
Thessalonians:

It is God's will that you should be sanctified: that you should
avoid sexual immorality; that each of you should learn to control your own body in a way that is holy and honorable, not
in passionate lust like the pagans, who do not know God; and

that in this matter no one should wrong or take advantage of a brother or sister. The Lord will punish all those who commit such sins, as we told you and warned you before. For God did not call us to be impure, but to live a holy life. Therefore, anyone who rejects this instruction does not reject a human being but God, the very God who gives you his Holy Spirit. (1 Thessalonians 4:3–8)

Learning to control our bodies is about formation.
Resisting pagan passions is about formation.
Honoring women is about formation.
Rejecting these commands leads to deformation.
The only answer is to reorder your desires—to reroute them.

## REORDERING OUR DESIRES

First, *God is trying to reorder our desires toward himself.* God is not trying to limit our desires; he is trying to direct them back to a divine source.

So much of the disillusionment of sex is that it doesn't ultimately meet the deepest longings we have. Yes, there is profound pleasure with sex. Yes, there can be moments of euphoria. But ultimately we are left wanting more when it's over. As Augustine noted, "For wherever the human soul turns itself, other than to you, it is fixed in sorrows, even if it is fixed upon beautiful things."[14]

99

Sorrowful sex—this describes the experience of so many men.

If we worship created things instead of the Creator, we are prone to profound disappointment. Sex has become a secular form of salvation seeking to save us from loneliness, save us from boredom, save us from ourselves. But what a sad heaven—this heaven that can reject you, betray you, crush you with your neediness and expectations. How fragile a salvation to turn sex into a god.

God is grieved at the attempts to find fulfillment outside himself:

> "Be appalled at this, you heavens, and shudder with great horror," declares the LORD. "My people have committed two sins: They have forsaken me, the spring of living water, and have dug their own cisterns, broken cisterns that cannot hold water." (Jeremiah 2:12–13)

Cisterns that can't hold water—broken and leaking.

There is no woman on earth who can hold the depth of love that you need.

There is no erotic encounter wild enough to satisfy your ache for transcendence.

There is no completing soulmate to give you the intimacy you crave.

Lesser loves always let us down. God wants to fulfill our desire with what truly satisfies. In fact, God is not afraid of our desires; he is saddened by the weakness of them. He wants us to hunger for more and refuse to settle for less. The search for sex is a search for something deeper—a disguised search for the divine. That's why G. K. Chesterton said, "Every man who knocks on the door of a brothel is looking for God."[15] Jesus seeks to invite us to that which will satisfy. Tim and Kathy Keller told us,

> To be loved but not known is comforting but superficial. To be known and not loved is our greatest fear. But to be fully known and truly loved is, well, a lot like being loved by God. It is what we need more than anything. It liberates us from pretense, humbles us out of our self-righteousness, and fortifies us for any difficulty life can throw at us.[16]

Jesus invites us to himself. "Come to me, all you who are weary and burdened, and I will give you rest" (Matthew 11:28). Rest from having to perform; rest from the need for constant recognition; rest for your adrenal glands and dopamine depleted brain; rest from your shame and addiction—Jesus offers real satisfaction for our deepest needs. "If anyone is thirsty, let him come to Me and drink. The one who believes in Me, as the Scripture said, 'From his innermost being will flow rivers of living water'" (John 7:37–38 NASB). He wants us to experience a flow of life from the core of who we are, rather than grasping and reaching for some erotic vapor.

God offered the fulfillment of what we want:

> "Come, all you who are thirsty, come to the waters; and you who have no money, come, buy and eat! Come, buy wine and milk without money and without cost. Why spend money on what is not bread, and your labor on what does not satisfy? Listen, listen to me, and eat what is good, and you will delight in the richest of fare." (Isaiah 55:1–2)

Jesus offers a salvation that is permanent not temporary, accepting not rejecting, empowering not addicting, transforming not shaming. Sex points beyond itself to the source of life and love, the source we have been seeking but struggle to name.

Second, *God is trying to reorder our desires for the good of others.* He is forming men who will respect women and stop treating them as a commodity—men who give relational commitment, rather than simply demanding sexual satisfaction—men who love, not lust.

In his classic work *The Four Loves*, C. S. Lewis shed light on the power and nature of love in four different aspects:

- *Storge*, the love of affection
- *Eros*, the love of romance
- *Philia*, the love of friendship
- *Agape*, the love of charity[17]

Because of the shadow of sexualization the Enemy has cast on the world, our ordering of these loves has been wrong. The world orders them this way:

1. Erotic love
2. Storge love
3. Philia love
4. Agape love

Our world today starts with sexual attraction and desire. It expects sex as soon as possible and without commitment. Then it looks for Storge love, that sense of wonder and nostalgia that makes us want to keep the other person around. Then it works on building a friendship to keep the connection permanent. Then, if all these conditions have been met, it decides to commit through agape love. But this is the opposite order of biblical love. No wonder so many relationships fall apart—they are built on the wrong foundation, one that can't sustain the stress, strains, and expectations of life.

But when God reorders our desires, he reorders our approach to relationships.

1. Agape love
2. Philia love
3. Storge love
4. Erotic love

We begin with considering the humanity of the other person and the divine image they bear, treating them with honor and respect. Then we build a friendship where we learn to love the actual person for who they are, not who we hope they can be. Then we learn to truly enjoy their presence with depth and wonder and joy. And finally, we consummate that union with erotic fulfillment based on a covenant.

For the believer, sex is not about how much you get, but how much you give. It's about a physical sign of a whole life commitment. It does with our bodies what we do with our lives—the sacrificial giving and uniting of our time, energy, attention, and resources. We let God's revolutionary love shape the pattern of our human love, not the animalistic lust of the sexual revolution.

## A COMMUNITY OF AGAPE IN A WORLD OF LUST

The church has so much work to do in repairing its vision for the world. But it can reach back into its past with great hope. In the first centuries, one of the most distinctive features of the church was its reformed desires, which shaped its vision of sex.

In an early piece of Christian writing from an unknown author, known simply as the "Epistle to Diognetus," we read, "[Christians] marry, as do all others. They beget children. . . . They have a common table, but not a common bed."[18]

A common table, but a sanctified bed.

A table where we can belong.

A table of respect and humanity, not commodification and abuse.

A table of healing and restoration.

A table of grace and transformation in a culture of shame.

A table of brothers and sisters, not predators and victims.

A table where Christ meets with his church in love.

## FROM A SHADOW TO A SIGN

Satan wants to blot out God with sex. He wants it to come between you and God so you can't see anything else. He wants you to elevate women into idols and view sex as your path to salvation. Then he wants to break your heart and addict you to pleasure. Then you will never lift your eyes beyond sex to the

God who created it, and you will hide in shame and struggle alone, fixed on your failure and regret.

We must rediscover that our quest for sex is ultimately not a quest for pleasure; it's a quest for union, a quest for belonging, a disguised search for God. Though we struggle to say it out loud as men, what we ache for is to be vulnerable and accepted, known and loved, seen and celebrated. Sexuality is a reminder of the true source of our acceptance and love. God became vulnerable for us.

Sex is a sign that points to the light of love, not a shadow that drowns us in hedonic shame. For a generation of men, the sexual revolution has failed us. But the clouds are starting to break, and the sun is coming out. A generation of men are turning their desires toward Jesus. We have a chance to become men who are satisfied in Jesus and serve others from the overflow of love.

• • •

I (Jon) am forty-six years old, and I am looking over a photo album from my life. At this point I live with few illusions about sex. I have been married for twenty-five years and know the pain and complexity of human love. Although my wife is a tremendous gift, she is not my savior. She doesn't even want to play that role. She would not want to be crushed under a weight only Christ himself can carry.

And truth be told, sex complicates rather than simplifies our relationship. But it has been a gift, one held in covenant and a shared life. It's been a reminder to reorder my love away from selfish lust to sacrificial care. It's been a formative gift of mutual submission and shared joy. But it's just a sign that points beyond the shadow of this world to the life of love we are all invited into: Christ himself, in whose presence is fullness of joy.

# THE SHADOW OF AMBITION

*The Lie:* Ambition is fuel for personal success.

*The Truth:* Ambition is a gift for kingdom impact.

*The best lack all conviction, while the worst*
*Are full of passionate intensity.*

**—WILLIAM BUTLER YEATS**


*A man's worth is no greater than*
*the worth of his ambitions.*

**—MARCUS AURELIUS**

**We know of no word that causes greater confu-**
sion in the hearts of men today than the word *ambition*. For some
it touches the deepest passion of the heart and shakes them out
of bed in the morning. For others it's a word that invokes shame
and obligation, naming another thing they lack. It can represent
another reminder that they don't have the definitive factor that
attracts women and earns respect with men.

It's hard for a man to know what to do with his ambition
these days because the channels for healthy expression seem to be
blocked. The word *ambition* can trigger vision and passion, or it
can paralyze and overwhelm. What exactly is a man to do with
his ambition? What do you do with yours?

Some argue that your ambition should focus on making an
impact—you should seek to make the largest difference possible

on the greatest amount of people. But often, when you look behind the scenes, there is a trail of wounded hearts and buried bodies at the price of success. In our desire to do great things, we can do great damage.

Some argue that we should focus on influence; we should seek to gain as wide an audience as possible; we should build a platform to distribute our perspective and positions; we should seek to mold and shape the views of others with the force of our lives. But change without direction is wasted energy. Change for change's sake can lead to exhaustion without progress.

Others suggest we should focus on none of these things. Ambition is toxic, they say. It's the driving factor in so much of the brokenness and pain in the world. History is the battlefield of ambition, and success is written with the blood of losers. And it seems there is some truth to this. The progress in our world today has come with unintended consequences. Kingdoms are often built with tears. Pastors use volunteers to build churches, influencers use followers to build platforms, brands use customers to build fortunes. So many of the calls for justice today are calls to acknowledge and repair the damage done by aggressive men who built their legacy without thought of the human cost.

## AMBITION AND SPIRITUALITY

Donald Whitney said, "One way to simplify your spirituality is to clarify your ambition."[1]

Have you examined your relationship to ambition as a man? It's not often talked about in the context of our faith, but what we want and how hard we chase it are at the core of our spiritual lives. You don't want to be paralyzed by fear and let your potential rot in

Ambition is not often talked about in the context of our faith, but what we want and how hard we chase it are at the core of our spiritual lives.

the soil of amusements, and you don't want to be an ego-driven jerk seeking success at any costs. Is it possible to cultivate godly ambition? Is it even good to wake the dragon of desire in our hearts?

## WORLDLY AMBITION

One of the cautions about ambition is the way it influences how we treat others. It can distort our perspective of those around us. It can force a competitive filter over all we say and do. James K. A. Smith noted that ambition in a worldly sense is defined by two main marks: domination and attention.[2]

Domination makes us feel like we must win at all costs. It's not enough for us to do our best; we have to measure ourselves against others. Only when our best is better than others' do we get a sense of accomplishment. When I (Jon) moved to the United States, one of the first things that struck me was the aggressive language surrounding success. When someone does well, we talk about them *killing* it, *crushing* it, *slaying* it. These words are heavy. Winner-loser, victory-defeat, life-death—aggression without compassion seems to be the price of success.

One of the most confusing things about the disciples in the Gospels was their desire to dominate. It seemed Jesus' personal

111

invitation to be his apostles was not enough. In Luke 22 this came into embarrassing focus. Jesus gathered his friends to celebrate the Passover, his last meal with them. He imbued his life into the meal, telling them the bread and body represented his gift to the world. He washed their feet as a servant of love.

And what was the disciples' response? Humility? Gratitude? No. Verse 24 notes, "A dispute also arose among them as to which of them was considered to be greatest." Their need for human greatness overshadowed the Messiah. Their need to dominate distorted their discipleship.

The second mark of worldly ambition is the need for recognition. In modern life it's not enough to win; we need an audience for our accomplishments. Timothy Dwight, president of Yale from 1886 to 1898, warned graduating students against this and the "love of distinction." He wrote, "But among all the passions which mislead, endanger, and harass the mind, none is more hostile to its peace, none more blind, none more delirious than the love of distinction."[3]

Dwight would be grieved at how much our modern world is built on seeking distinction. Ambition demands attention, and to get attention we must distinguish ourselves from the masses. This introduces a comparative and performative element in all we do. A whole generation of men has been raised on the need for distinction. In a recent study, 86 percent of young Americans said they want to be social media influencers—kill and crush, notice and narcissism, domination and recognition—a delirious pursuit to post everything online.

The shadow of ambition is standing tall over a generation of men.

## RESISTING AMBITION

With so much damage done by worldly ambition, it may seem wise for Christians to banish it from our lives. Maybe we should focus on other virtues that don't cause so much damage. But Smith noted this kind of overaction can do its own kind of damage:

> If you keep walking around the phenomenon of ambition, you'll start to note a couple of features. First, the opposite of ambition is not humility; it is sloth, passivity, timidity, and complacency. We sometimes like to comfort ourselves by imagining that the ambitious are prideful and arrogant so that those of us who never risk, never aspire, never launch out into the deep get to wear the moralizing mantle of humility. But this imagining is often just thin cover for a lack of courage, even laziness. Playing it safe isn't humble.[4]

The truth is when it comes to your life, you are not at war *with* ambition; you are in a war *for* ambition—godly ambition. Without godly ambition you will collapse back into a cocoon of self. Without godly ambition your vision will be reduced to your own wants and needs. You won't recognize it, but instead of seeking first the kingdom of God, you will seek the kingdom of the American dream.

God has more for you than shallow ambition and a worldly version of success. God has more for you than a life of false humility and shallow pursuits. God wants to fill you with a soul-stirring kind of holy ambition. So how do we convert worldly ambition into holy ambition, and who can guide us along the way?

## NEHEMIAH, KINGDOM VISION,
## AND HOLY AMBITION

The thing about Nehemiah that makes him the right mentor on ambition is how normal he seemed. Nehemiah wasn't a priest, wasn't a pastor, wasn't a Levite. Nehemiah worked in the government as a cupbearer for the king. Nehemiah was a man living his life, working his job, trying to stay out of trouble. He served in Susa, the winter residence of the Persian kings.

He was a long way from Jerusalem and the exiles who had returned to the land. You probably remember that God had judged his people for their corruption and compromise, and Jerusalem had been destroyed by Nebuchadnezzar. After seventy years of exile, a remnant had returned, but they were in mourning and distress. The city was in ruins and the people were struggling. But for all intents and purposes, there wasn't really anything Nehemiah could do, or was required to do, about the problems they faced.

But it turned out, just like God placed Esther in power to save her people, and he also moved Joseph to Egypt to rescue the people of his day, God put Nehemiah in the perfect place to rebuild the ruins and remove the reproach of his people. Nehemiah just needed ambition to activate his potential, and this happened by asking a simple question.

I (Jon) have heard my friend Pastor Sam Gibson say countless times that "the questions we ask determine the culture we create." Our questions determine our focus, and our focus determines our future. And Nehemiah's question ended up being the inciting incident that dragged him into a story he never saw coming.

In Nehemiah 1:2 we read, "I [Nehemiah] questioned them about the Jewish remnant that had survived the exile, and also about Jerusalem."

The answer Nehemiah received about what was happening in Jerusalem was tragic. Reading on, verse 3 says, "They said to me, 'Those who survived the exile and are back in the province are in great trouble and disgrace. The wall of Jerusalem is broken down, and its gates have been burned with fire.'"

To be honest, when I think about the questions I ask, they are often just about me. My questions focus on my goals, my desires, my wants. The prophet Jeremiah lamented that people failed to ask the right questions. He asked, "Who will have pity on you, Jerusalem? Who will mourn for you? Who will stop to ask how you are?" (Jeremiah 15:5).

Nehemiah was showing his heart connecting beyond his own time and place, beyond his own comfort and position. He was allowing his heart to be affected by the cries of another generation. And while he didn't know it at the time, his question would unlock the key to cultivating holy ambition.

Instead of Jerusalem being a city on a hill and a light for the world, it was a struggling community in squalor and ruin. Once a center of worship and wonder, Jerusalem was now an embarrassment and disgrace. The wall was broken down and the gates were burned. The people couldn't defend themselves from their enemies or protect their families. They were fragile, vulnerable, and covered with shame.

To be honest, my response would have been very different than Nehemiah's. I would have felt bad for the remnant, but I would have returned to my life. I might have added them to my prayer list before getting back to my job. I would have felt sorry for them but not enough to do anything for them.

But Nehemiah was drawn beyond the horizon of his own concerns. He looked a little higher than the men of his time and saw beyond the walls of selfishness to the work God wanted to do in the world. Nehemiah lifted his eyes beyond his kingdom to God's kingdom. His vision moved from personal concern to God's concern. If we are going to be men who convert worldly ambition to holy ambition, we are going to have to lift our eyes beyond the boundaries of our own concerns as well.

## LEARNING TO ASK KINGDOM QUESTIONS

All of us draw a line around our own interests and affairs. We determine who we are responsible for and tend to ignore the rest. We put our heads down, take care of our own, let others deal with those on the outside. Unless we are personally impacted by tragedy, we don't care about tragedy, not really.

In his book *A Christian Manifesto*, Francis Schaeffer warned of a looming threat to the church. It wasn't the huge culture wars we think of today; it was something smaller, more insidious. It was a reduction of kingdom vision to personal vision. He warned about reducing our faith to "personal peace and affluence."[5] When Christian men stop caring about God's kingdom and mission, and reduce their vision to personal well-being and wealth, the church is doomed. A man must live for more than himself and his stuff.

It seems whole generations of Christians failed to heed

Schaeffer's warning. Our prayers and desires look remarkably like the wishes and wants of those who don't know God. We have changed God's concerns to personal concerns. We are bending our faith around ourselves. Take the Lord's Prayer, for example. Since the days of the church fathers, it's been pointed out that the first three requests in the Lord's Prayer focus on matters that concern God—the glory of his name, the coming of his kingdom, and the accomplishing of his will—while the last three requests deal with the needs of the one who is praying—the necessities of life, personal forgiveness of sin, and victory over trial and temptation.

Jesus gave us this prayer to orient our vision and order our desire. In praying the Lord's Prayer, our hearts are drawn up into what God is doing in the world. It lifts us beyond the horizon of our own concerns and engages us in the story of God's will and work. It looks something like this:

- The Father's name
- The Father's kingdom
- The Father's will

*Then*

- My needs
- My forgiveness
- My protection

This prayer elevates a man's vision to something noble, something helpful, something large. It pulls him out of the cocoon of self into a kingdom calling.

But so often our ambition is reduced and redirected back to ourselves. The gravity of sin draws our circle of concern tightly. Our vision and prayer collapse inward. Instead of our lives being used to build God's kingdom, we ask him to build ours. The prayer is then prayed like this:

- My provision
- My protection
- My forgiveness

*Then*

- The Father's name
- The Father's will
- The Father's kingdom

Personal peace and affluence draw a small circle around our lives. By pursuing greatness, we collapse into selfishness. That's why Philippians 2:3 pleads with us to "do nothing out of selfish ambition or vain conceit." Ungodly ambition destroys community, commodifies love, and turns brothers into opponents. As we saw in Nehemiah's story, you can measure a man's vision by the questions he asks. Kingdom questions lead to kingdom vision. Selfish questions lead to a smaller life.

Almost every week I (Jon) walk past Times Square Church in New York City. It's one of the largest churches in the city and serves the poor and hurting in a remarkable way. It meets in a historic theater, and the properties it owns are worth tens of millions. But it didn't start this way. David Wilkerson, the founding pastor of this church, was a minister leading a small congregation of around two hundred folks in rural Pennsylvania. The pressures of ministry were hard, and he used to relax at night by watching TV.

One night he got convicted about how much time he spent sitting in front of the screen. He asked a simple question, but one that would rock his world: "How much time am I spending in front of the TV each night?" Then a thought came to him. *What if I sold the TV and spent that time praying?*[6]

In February 1958, while seeking God in prayer, Wilkerson felt drawn to a copy of *Life* magazine. He came across the murder trial of a young polio victim who had been brutally stabbed to death by seven young gang members. Heartbroken by the crime, he asked another question: *How could this happen?*

He couldn't put the magazine down. His question led to a commission. He sensed God prompt him, "You've got to help those boys." At thirty years old, with no experience and no real plan, he drove to the trial in New York City to share the gospel with the gang members. He was removed from court and was mockingly photographed while holding a Bible. This image made its way to the front cover of the newspapers the next day.

But though the news reports were intended to mock this sup- posedly naïve young preacher, Wilkerson's actions earned him respect with the gang members, who recognized him from the publicity. He started to preach and witness on the streets, seeing radical conversions of some of the most violent gang members, most notably Nicky Cruz. Wilkerson's account of his experience was turned into a book called *The Cross and the Switchblade*, which sold tens of millions of copies. To help these kids get off drugs he started Teen Challenge, which has grown into an international movement around the world.

I remember reading that book as a new Christian in Australia, weeping with amazement at how God called a young pastor out of his comfort and into the front lines of the kingdom of God. It all started because of a question. Little did I know I would eventually end up in New York too.

When I stop in front of Times Square Church today, my heart is full of gratitude that a pastor in a small rural church asked a kingdom question. That question opened his eyes to what God was doing in the world. It starts by asking what God wants, not what we want. It starts by asking him to give us his heart. Holy ambition starts with kingdom vision.

**Holy ambition starts with kingdom vision.**

If you are going to be a man of holy ambition, you must learn to ask questions that lift your eyes and expose your heart— questions whose answers may very well implicate you and call you into action, questions that connect you to the needs of those around you.

Where are that kid's parents?

Why are our neighborhoods designed like this?

What should we do with the Christmas bonus this year?

Why do I live where I live?

What should I do with my spare time?

Why is the youth group so small?

Why are the men at work so discouraged?

Why are kids so anxious?

My friend Sarah asked a kingdom question that changed her life. She asked, "What would happen if we took the teachings of Jesus seriously and didn't water them down?" The answer led her to move to the poorest neighborhood in her city and start a ministry called A House on Beekman, serving and empowering kids in the South Bronx.[7]

My friend Gareth asked why so many high school guys were missing from his church. Now on Sunday nights about fifty young men fill his house for pizza, discipleship, and spiritual formation.

My friend Tyler asked why the church lagged so far behind the world in terms of creativity and entrepreneurship. He started Missional Labs to cultivate and empower entrepreneurship within the church.[8]

Change the questions you ask, and you may change your life. Allow God to expand your circle of concern, and you never know where heaven will break in. And when heaven breaks in, the shadow of selfish ambition shrinks back in the light.

## THE CRYSTALLIZATION OF DISCONTENT

Many people ask questions that open their eyes to the kingdom of God, but not all of them step through the door. When Nehemiah found out about the state of God's people in Jerusalem, something shifted in his spirit. His eyes were opened and his heart was broken. Look at chapter 1, verse 4: "When I heard these things, I sat down and wept. For some days I mourned and fasted and prayed before the God of heaven."

These are strong words. Weeping and mourning come from

a broken heart. Holy ambition is fueled by sacred tears. We need men who weep in our world today, men marked with the gift of tears. Fasting was required of the Jews only once a year, on the annual Day of Atonement (Leviticus 16:29), but Nehemiah was desperate to identify with his people.

It's worth noting that this wasn't just an emotional moment; Nehemiah was cut to the core. If you check the timeline in this passage, Nehemiah felt this burden for four months. It's one thing for something to get *to* you, another thing when it gets *in* you. Pain can pass through us, or pain can propel us. It can lead to passivity, or it can lead to resolve.

Something happened in Nehemiah's pain, something remarkable. It's called "the crystallization of discontent."[9] This phrase describes what happens inside someone when they get fed up.

It's the moment you realize you can't take it anymore.

It's the interior moment of resolve before the external moment of change.

It's the settling of the heart before the shaking of a life.

It's the moment you see yourself in a photo after you've put on forty pounds and say, "Heck no," before you get back to the gym.

It's the moment you decide to break up with a woman who devalues you, when you have been making excuses for her for years.

It's the moment you realize, right before you quit, that you are stuck in a dead-end job and they are never going to take you seriously.

Every breakthrough in history has been preceded by someone experiencing the crystallization of discontent.

It's Polycarp, before his trial, refusing to deny Jesus.[10]
It's Rosa Parks on the bus refusing to go to the back.
It's the addict who realizes "this is bottom" before he goes
    to his first meeting.
It's Jesus in the garden sweating blood before the cross.
It could be you picking up this book, refusing to drift
    through the rest of your days.

The crystallization of discontent is one of the greatest gifts a man can experience, because it's the fuel for radical change. But it must be carefully guarded, because the Enemy will work to shut it down and eliminate the threat.

He will work to get you to *doubt* your discontent. He will whisper things like, "Are you sure you really want to make a change? Are you sure you have the emotional energy for this?" He will tell you this isn't a good time; you aren't that kind of person, and it's not worth the criticism you will face.

He will work to *distract* you from your discontent.

When a man gets a burden to change, a thousand issues will spontaneously arise. Some will be negative—relational conflicts, work challenges, plumbing issues, anything. Or simple pleasures will have numbing effects: the show you have been waiting for finally comes out; your friends get a lake house but can't use if for the summer—they want to know if you'd like it? Almost anything will do if it dampens your urgency. It's amazing how a good pizza and Netflix series can bleed the ambition from a man's heart.

And he will work to *dismiss* your discontent.

Psychologists have a fancy term to describe our ability to get used to what's happening around us. They call it habituation. We normalize what used to traumatize. We get used to mass shootings, used to pornography, used to debt, used to the brokenness all around us. I always think of that scene in the movie *Hotel Rwanda* where the cameras show up and capture the beginning of the genocide. A Rwandan man asks a reporter how the world could fail to intervene when they witness such atrocities. The reporter replies: "I think if people see this footage they'll say, 'Oh my God, that's horrible,' then go on eating their dinners."[11]

Satan wants to dismiss the conviction in your heart as unrealistic and unnecessary. He tells us, "This is just the way the world is, and there isn't much someone like you can do to change it. What are we having for dinner again?"

## FEEDING YOUR FRUSTRATION

Several years back I (Jon) struggled through a season of deep sadness. I was going through a complex and frustrating time of church leadership. There were tensions and criticism, and I felt powerless and stuck. I had two teenagers in the house dealing with the challenges of trying to follow Jesus in New York and a living situation in Manhattan that was horrifically unsustainable. I was overwhelmed and exhausted, and passivity had set in.

I have a high pain threshold, which helps me endure hardship but often hinders flourishing. I didn't have enough energy to face my problems, but I had enough energy to mitigate them. This is a dangerous place for a man. I eventually went to see a mentor who is part therapist, part counselor and friend.

I poured out my heart to him, laid the issues out, and awaited his response. I don't know if I was expecting an encouraging word or an awkward hug, but I got neither.

"You need to get angry," he said. "Really angry. You need to feed your frustration, poke at your problems, and sit in your sadness till you think you are going to snap. Then when you have reached that point of anger, you need to work to keep and cultivate it. Then you will have a new kind of energy to get out of the mud you are stuck in that is making you miserable. When you move forward, the sadness will lift, and you will find yourself in a new season."

I went home and told my wife what he said. Her response shocked me too.

"Good. I've been waiting for something to wake you up. It's time for us to move forward."

If you want to convert your worldly ambition to holy ambition, you are going to have to feed your frustration. You are going to have to let the brokenness of the world into your heart. You are going to have to marinate your disconnect in sacred tears. You have to refuse to doubt, be distracted by the trivial, or be numbed by the pain. The fuel you need will come from the frustration you feel. You need to get angry. You need to stop normalizing what is traumatizing. You need to bring your anguish to God and ask him what to do.

But beware: as Nehemiah found out, what he asks may astound you.

## RADICAL SACRIFICIAL ACTION

Eugene Peterson wrote,

> Be slow to pray. Praying puts us at risk of getting involved with God's conditions. Praying most often doesn't get us what we want but what God wants, something quite at variance with what we conceive to be in our best interests. And when we realize what is going on, it is often too late to go back.[12]

This exact thing happened to Nehemiah. He found himself perfectly positioned to respond to the things that had broken his heart. He saw the kingdom vision with clarity. He felt the people burdened with urgency, but now he had to act. He had to take massive, sacrificial action, and there was no turning back.

Many men struggle to take massive action. We do things once or twice, and then get discouraged when nothing happens. But we live in a world of resistance. You won't move forward without a fight. That's where massive action comes in.

There are four degrees of action men can take:

- Doing nothing
- Retreating
- Taking normal levels of action
- Taking massive action

Most men's actions fall into the first three categories. But your life will not change until you focus on the fourth level. We love sharing our opinions, critiquing, and judging, but the men the world needs are men who act.

The first action Nehemiah took was toward God.

## MASSIVE ACTION IN PRAYER

Jocko Willink is famous for talking about "extreme ownership."[13] It's the idea that it may not be your fault, but it is your responsibility. Though Nehemiah didn't cause the problems in Jerusalem, he understood the principle of ownership. He knew there is no authority without responsibility. He took responsibility for the rebellion of the people and owned it before God.

His prayers were prayers of identification:

> I confess the sins we Israelites, including myself and my father's family, have committed against you. We have acted very wickedly toward you. We have not obeyed the commands, decrees and laws you gave your servant Moses. (Nehemiah 1:6–7)

We live in a society that often rejects group identification. We reject responsibility for the sins of previous generations or the faults of our fathers. Nehemiah knew change comes from identifying with the past, not ignoring it. He wasn't trying to beat himself up or signal virtue to others. He knew he had to acknowledge his guilt before God if he was going to have favor with God.

He started praying prayers of promise:

LORD, the God of heaven, the great and awesome God, who keeps his covenant of love with those who love him and keep his commandments. (v. 5)

Nehemiah didn't limit what was possible to his own capacity; he called on God to act according to his covenant of love.

"But if you return to me and obey my commands, then even if your exiled people are at the farthest horizon, I will gather them from there and bring them to the place I have chosen as a dwelling for my Name." (v. 9)

So many men fall back into apathy or scramble to achieve because they fail to secure the favor of heaven. They hustle and grind and push and strive because they have no assurance that God is on their side. Godly change comes when men take massive action before God.

## MASSIVE ACTION IN THE WORLD

We live in a world of disruptive leadership. Entrepreneurs are always trying to disrupt industries with the latest technology and innovation. Nehemiah acted with such massive action that we still feel the effects of his disruption today:

- Nehemiah asked King Artaxerxes for permission to rebuild the wall of Jerusalem (Nehemiah 2:5). This was a massive risk to ask someone to rebuild a city that could become a military and economic threat.

- He asked the king to overthrow a longstanding foreign policy against Judah, asking for favorable terms when he had zero bargaining power to do so (vv. 7–8).
- Nehemiah asked the king for the supplies to rebuild the wall (v. 8). This may be one of the most audacious requests in ancient history.
- He asked the king for travel permits and protection along the way (v. 7).
- He won the people's hearts with servant-oriented leadership (chap. 3). Nehemiah led from the front, mixing passionate prayer and hard labor.
- He overcame resistance and opposition that included violence and ridicule (chaps. 4–6). He refused to be intimidated or give in to criticism and fear. He was convinced he was doing a great work and refused to come down.
- He helped facilitate a national revival and gave the attention to Ezra the priest to lead the people properly (chaps. 8–13). This was a time of celebration and rejoicing that could be heard for miles around.
- He helped renew the covenant of God with his people (chaps. 7–10).
- He celebrated the Feast of Booths (8:13–18).
- He helped reorganize and repopulate the city (chaps. 11–12).

Nehemiah was a spiritual, strategic, strong, and servant-hearted man.

We remember Nehemiah as a God-made man, not a self-made man.

## HOLY AMBITION LEADS TO
## DIVINE ACCELERATION

When a man is filled with holy ambition, anything is possible. Holy ambition leads to divine acceleration. When Nehemiah was seized with a kingdom vision, he experienced the crystallization of his discontent, took radical action, and saw the implausible become possible. He rallied the people to build the walls—two miles in circumference and wide enough for a choir to walk around—in just fifty-two days. Holy ambition accomplished more in fifty-two days than the previous fifty-two years:

> So the wall was completed on the twenty-fifth of the month Elul, in fifty-two days. When all our enemies heard about it, and all the nations surrounding us saw it, they lost their confidence; for they realized that this work had been accomplished with the help of our God. (6:15–16 NASB)

Before God gets ready to move in your life, he is going to clarify your ambition. He wants to free you from small vision, save you from scrambling and striving, and help you build a legacy that lasts for eternity. Kingdom vision plus the crystallization of discontent, plus radical action, are the keys to holy ambition.

## JESUS: HOLY AMBITION EMBODIED

Our vision of holy ambition is rooted deeply in what it means to be a disciple, because Jesus was a man seized with holy ambition.

Jesus didn't just rebuild a wall; he is rebuilding the world. He resisted the need for domination and recognition when he faced the Enemy in the wilderness. Jesus lifted his eyes beyond the boundaries of his own concern, to the plight of fallen humanity, including you. And he experienced the crystallization of discontent.

He refused to sit by and watch a dying world perish. He shed sacred tears when his friend died, and he wept over Jerusalem's rebellion. He took extreme ownership for the sins of humanity, even though sin wasn't his fault. He identified with us and took our burden as his own. He took massive sacrificial action—dying for our sins, defeating death, and rising again in power. He is seated at the right hand of the Father, and he lives to intercede for us, even now.

Worldly ambition can be a curse. It feeds our egos, compromises our integrity, damages our relationships, and fills us with pride. But holy ambition is a gift. It's an advantage for men in our world today. It clarifies our vision, stirs our passion, activates heaven, and disrupts the brokenness of our world.

Our vision is to see you rise into your full calling, to reach your redemptive potential.

May God help you ask better questions.
May God lift your vision beyond the horizon of your own
    concerns.
May God help you feed your frustration.
May God call you to covenantal prayer.
May God give you courage to make impossible asks.
May God accelerate his purposes through your life.

May you see decades unfold in mere days, for the God of
heaven is on your side.

May you push back the shadow of worldly ambition and
leave a legacy of brilliant light.

# THE SHADOW OF FUTILITY

*The Lie:* My work doesn't matter.

*The Truth:* You have a calling to serve and heal the world.

*A [man] should be able to change a diaper, plan an invasion, butcher a hog, conn a ship, design a building, write a sonnet, balance accounts, build a wall, set a bone, comfort the dying, take orders, give orders, cooperate, act alone, solve equations, analyze a new problem, pitch manure, program a computer, cook a tasty meal, fight efficiently, die gallantly. Specialization is for insects.*

**—ROBERT ANSON HEINLEIN**

**According to an article in the *New York Times*,** "Hundreds of thousands of men in their late thirties and early forties stopped working during the pandemic and have lingered on the labor market's sidelines since."[1]

Andy Crouch's observation about the three large shifts that have driven the development of our modern world over the last thousand years seems relevant here. He talked about "three expansions of power."[2]

The first occurred in 1397 when, in Florence, Italy, the first bank was created, setting in motion a shift from "wealth as land" to "wealth as money."

The second shift, in 1769, was the invention of the steam engine. Work changed forever. Work once done by bodies was increasingly accomplished by machines.

The third shift occurred in 1948 when Claude Shannon

published his landmark paper *A Mathematical Theory of Communication*, which set in motion a new age where knowledge is no longer based on wisdom but on information.

All three of these things represent disconnects.

Whereas wealth was once embedded in something you could touch and feel—the home you lived in and the land you worked—it was now wrapped up almost entirely in bits of metal and paper to which we'd assigned value, or, in the modern world, small pieces of plastic that electronically send this abstract wealth from one account to another.

Whereas we once prioritized wisdom as the hard-won reward of a lifetime of experience, we now live in a world where everyone has an unfathomable amount of information at their fingertips.

And while many people still perform manual labor, many of the most highly valued jobs involve sitting at a computer and pressing keys on a keyboard, with results that often aren't tangible. Our work, our lives, and even *ourselves* can feel like cogs in an abstract machine, rather than forming a holistic, meaningful reality.

In a world like that, identity, meaning, and purpose can feel hard to come by.

And it can be especially tough to believe that the work we do is genuinely meaningful—which is when the shadow of futility starts to fall over a man's heart. As men, we need to see our work as meaningful and substantive. We want to believe that we're making a difference in the world. But when so much of the modern world is geared toward disconnection, abstraction, and systems that seem like they will carry on with or without us, an overwhelming sense of futility is always lurking.

Let's talk about it. Let's get equipped to fight the shadow of futility. The truth is the struggle for meaning and purpose is not new—it just looks different today than it used to. But even with all the changes, the funda-

The truth is the struggle for meaning and purpose is not new—it just looks different today than it used to.

mental principles for overcoming futility and finding meaning in our work remain just as valid today as they ever were—you just need to know where to look.

## THE CALL TO RULE

There are levels of mastery to a man's life, and if he tries to skip a step, it implodes the next one. Let me (Jeff) explain.

Men and women were commanded by God to rule. We are co-laborers and teammates. What I'm about to say is just as true for women as for men, but this is a book directed to men so I want to focus on the specific ways men are called to rule—and the ways we tend to struggle with that calling.

There are four levels of ruling. Think of them like concentric circles.

1. Ruling yourself
2. Ruling a small team (marriage)
3. Ruling a tribe
4. Ruling a city[3]

You can't, or rather shouldn't, level up to the next without first mastering the one before.

Let's take the first one: *Rule yourself.* This is what differentiates boys from men. Boys are ruled by their passions, lusts, dreams, people's praise or critique, money, and so on. Becoming a man requires developing mastery over those things by channeling their energy toward a specific focus—that doesn't destruct but produces. Learning to rule yourself begins in childhood and tends to continue through young adulthood.

I (Jeff) was dominated by so much energy and passion as a young adult. But getting married at a young age—twenty-two—forced me to realize I had to master my energy and passion or it was going to have destructive consequences.

I aggressively pursued my own growth. I logged hours with mentors who helped me rule rather than be ruled by the things I wanted. I took years to rewire my brain's approach to all kinds of hopes and desires. It was hard work to master my passions and it took so much time—but it was necessary. I would not have been able to rule in my marriage or my work without learning to rule myself first.

If you don't learn to rule in the domain of the season you are currently called to, you will bring destruction into the next one.

Do you have massive childhood wounds you haven't dealt with? Have you failed to rule yourself and then tried to rule in the areas of marriage or another small team? Yeah, that's a ticking time bomb.

Do you have a marriage filled with unhealed jealousy, hurt, and selfishness, but you are trying to go out and be a leader of your city? Destruction.

It's helpful to ask, What season am I in? Have I skipped mastery in the previous one? That's the quickest way to find a land mine under the surface in your life.

Work sits right in the middle of all this. It's our way and place to rule, to bring order and beauty out of chaos, to defend the boundaries of light, to take ground one inch at a time over the borders of darkness. That's what your work is for. Do you see it that way?

If you are battling feelings of futility in the work you are doing, your first move should not be to look for another job. Instead, check those levels of rule. Have you learned to rule yourself, or are you being dominated by your passions and by others' perceptions of you? If you are married, are you leading your family well? Chances are that getting those things in order will go a long way toward helping you overcome feelings of futility in whatever work you have been called to.

## THE SACREDNESS OF WORK

When I (Jeff) was in my twenties, I was working in the video space, producing content on YouTube. When I finally had a video pop and got some traction, the path began to open up and I could see a lane I could run in.

But most of my mentors advised me against it.

"Jeff, I think you should be a pastor."
"You should plant a church."
"You should work at a church."

These were all great things, to be clear.
But I knew they weren't what I was supposed to do. I felt

a strong calling to the front lines of culture. In many ways, YouTube is the public square for the exchange of ideas and debate and conversation.

But it wasn't technically a ministry.

It felt second rate—JV—not as good.

I felt like there was a huge disconnect between what I felt called to do and the sense of meaning I wanted to feel in the work I was doing. The voices of some of my mentors and the implicit messages I'd heard in the church led me to suspect that I wasn't doing something meaningful.

But I learned that meaningfulness is found in *how* you do something, not just in *what* you do. And we as men need to recover the sacredness of daily work, in any domain.

It makes me think of a friend, one of the greatest pastors I know—except he's not technically a pastor; he's a businessman who owns several trampoline parks. But he uses his business as a vehicle for what amounts to pastoral ministry. He takes young men who are struggling with dire circumstances and gives them a couch to sleep on. He offers interest-free loans to people with needs. He invites single moms to come to the trampoline park before open hours for free so their kids can play while they get some time to rest or work.

> I learned that meaningfulness is found in *how* you do something, not just in *what* you do.

This friend of mine has counseled people through tough family circumstances, used the business to host free charity events or worship nights, and done so much more. Love, justice, blessing, and goodness radiate from his life. He is a man fully alive, ruling and reigning with what he has. He is a man who has walked out of the shadow of futility and is living in the light of his calling. His work may seem mundane to some—but it's utterly sacred.

## THE CALL TO FREEDOM

There are two valuable concepts I (Jeff) am constantly applying to my work:

- Dots versus circles
- Calling versus assignments

### Dots Versus Circles

You want to know the quickest way to feel paralyzed as a follower of God? See God's will as a dot. When you see God's will as a tiny speck, you imagine that to "be in God's will" you must hit a very specific bullseye.

*What job should I take?*

*Who should I marry?*

*What should I give my life to?*

When you see God's will as a dot, you may feel that even if you *barely miss*, you've still missed. Anything other than a bullseye is a failure. And the frustration adds up. When you live with constant concern that you're not in God's exact, specific will, it drains your energy and warps how you see your life.

But what if God's will is more like a circle? A sandbox to play in rather than a bullseye you need to hit every single time? In a sandbox, you can play in this corner or that corner, but you are still in the sandbox. The point is that you don't want to step out of the sandbox. But there's a lot of freedom within that sandbox, right?

Living in God's will brings us options and freedom, within a range that's defined not so much by the bullseyes we hit but by the big parameters of obedience to godly principles paired with right motives.

Here's another way to look at it. Imagine if a dad said, "You need to go to this school, marry this person, take this job," and so on. We'd call that dad controlling. But a dad who is in a relationship with you, constantly watching you, and giving you freedom to make decisions under his supervision and guidance? A father who, when he notices you making some bad decisions, lovingly nudges you back toward the sandbox? That's a good father.

Doesn't this sound like the garden of Eden, the kind of freedom God always intended for humans? He provided a whole garden to play in—just one tree forbidden to eat from. Tons of freedom and choice, with specific boundaries.

You as a man need to know there is someone more powerful than you, smarter than you, more loving than you, more knowledgeable than you—and he is actively guiding you. He is smiling down on you and helping you through life.

## Calling Versus Assignments

*Calling* is a word we hear a lot in Christian circles. And frankly I hate how often it is misused.

*What's your calling?*

*Where has God called you?*

These are big questions that often paralyze us because we

seldom get a specific answer. But no wonder we run into trouble here: we are confusing calling with assignments.

Calling is large. Calling is the gifting over your life—the wiring, the way you operate in the world. Calling is the thing friends or people around you constantly ask you about. It's the collection of ideas and activities you are most passionate about. It's the theme that has been woven into your DNA. Your calling is more like the circle than the dot—the sandbox rather than the bullseye.

In other words, calling isn't a specific job. This is where people run into trouble. They want their calling to be specific. But when you expect to receive crystal-clear instructions from God to pursue a specific job, there's a good chance you are setting yourself up for disillusionment and frustration.

Take my story above. People saw lots of gifts and passions in my life that seemed suited for ministry—so they assumed that being a pastor was my calling. But my calling is wider and deeper than that specific job. My calling includes having a prophetic voice that gets people to rethink how they are doing things in their normal lives. My calling is to be a "status quo shaker upper," as one of my friends used to say.

And guess what?

There are a million different assignments for that calling. Within the sandbox of having a prophetic voice and disrupting the status quo, there are plenty of different bullseyes that are legitimate options.

You may not have a specific assignment right now. If you *do* have one, you can trust that God will make it super clear to you. But you definitely have a calling. And finding your calling doesn't necessarily involve receiving a sign or some sort of definitive communication from God. Just pay attention to the way he's wired you. Notice your gifts and passions. Listen to the things godly people say about you and the things that make your heart come alive. Then go play in that sandbox. If you are in the right sandbox, you will be ready when your assignment becomes clear.

### Codes and Kairos

When Rick Rescorla called his best friend Dan to see if he was watching the events unfolding on September 11, 2001, Rick was standing on the forty-fourth floor of the south tower of the World Trade Center.

A plane had just crashed into the north tower, and Dan could see smoke from his window. The intercoms in the south tower were blaring a message: "Remain calm and remain in the building. Do not evacuate." This message was intended to help avoid pandemonium. No one realized that a second plane was just minutes away from crashing into the south tower. No one imagined these buildings were about to collapse.

But Rick, who as the vice president of corporate security for Morgan Stanley was responsible for the safety of hundreds of people in the building, ignored the command. He thought staying in the building was the dumbest thing possible. He made the decision to defy the order. Grabbing a megaphone, he started calmly telling people to evacuate. Both towers collapsed later that day. Rick saved 2,694 employees. Staggering.

Rick was among those who did not survive. He was last seen going up the stairs to make a final sweep.

As I read about Rick's life, a few things stood out to me.

First, he was built for that moment. He had been actively

training for it his whole life, both during his time in the military and in his roles in the security sector. In fact, he was obsessed with the hero narrative and being prepared.

Just a week earlier, on September 5, he'd sent an email to his friend Bill Shucart, who was head of neurosurgery at Boston University. In that email, he talked about a *kairos* moment—which is a Greek word that basically means "time" but carries the connotation of a moment with great significance.

"I have accepted the fact there will never be a kairos moment for me, just an uneventful Miltonian plow-the-fields discipline . . . a few more cups of mocha grande at Starbucks, each one losing a little bit more of its flavor," he wrote.[4]

Six days later, Rick's kairos moment arrived.

Rick's wife, in an interview after the fateful events of 9/11 that took the life of her husband and so many others, said, "He lived by a code. He had his own philosophy and he used to say to me, 'You declare what you're about when you're young and you try to stay on that road so that at the end of your life you knew you did the very best you could.'"[5]

Rick lived by a code. And because of that, he was ready when his kairos moment showed up. The code is what comes out in crisis. The code is what saves lives. The code is the North Star of purpose.

## WHAT'S YOUR CODE?

Too many men today *overemphasize* their specific job's role in bringing meaning and purpose to their lives, and they *underemphasize* the importance of the code they live by. But we need men with codes. You need a North Star to define your direction, a purpose to dedicate yourself to. You don't get the luxury of finding a code when disaster hits. It must already be there, embedded deep in your soul, if it's going to have any effectiveness in a moment of crisis.

N. T. Wright talked about this using the language of virtue, character, and a "second nature."[6] He mentioned the pilot Chesley "Sully" Sullenberger, who famously made a few flash decisions to land his plane on the Hudson River after a bird strike shortly after takeoff. Sully was only able to make that lifesaving decision because of his years of training. Staying calm in a moment of crisis had become "second nature." He didn't have to deliberate or wonder. His mind and heart were prepared to take decisive, effective action.

> We need men with codes.

Without intentional training or formation, men's second nature is not directed toward love, life, goodness, sacrifice, beauty, and goodness; it is more likely to be loneliness, shame, cowardice, and selfishness. But when men who live by a code are squeezed by a crisis or a challenge, they leak out virtues at every seam. Men who live by a code can change the world.

## THE IMPORTANCE OF PLAY

Before we close this chapter on the shadow of futility and all the ways you can infuse your work with deep meaning, we need to look at things from another angle. For many men, there are seasons in which work is not just meaningful to them—it becomes their everything. They find their work so compelling, with their identity so wrapped up in what they're accomplishing and the accolades they receive, that they begin to lose sight of everything else. And let me tell you, that's also a path to futility. If your work feels pointless, that's obviously a bad thing for your soul. But it can be just as harmful if your work consumes you.

I (Jeff) had a season not too long ago where everything seemed to be clicking. I was working hard. I had found my purpose. I knew what my assignment was. My life seemed to be packed with meaning. That should have kept the shadow of futility at bay, right?

But I was working tons of hours. When I took off the work hat and put on the father hat, I was starting from empty. I wanted to give my heart and time and energy to my kids, but they were getting the scraps.

I started to struggle, in part because I couldn't really point to something I was doing wrong. I wasn't working *that much*, I told myself. I was still seeing the kids; I was just tired.

But "tired" wasn't quite right—more like exhausted. I was burned out, to be honest. But I didn't want to think that work was the problem, so I just stayed stuck in that zone, unable to pinpoint and solve my own problems. And when I have problems I can't define or solve, I get anxious.

Before long, I started to wither on the vine. I was walking through each day with my eyes glazed over.

My first attempt to solve the issue was to go harder into spiritual disciplines. *Get up a little earlier. Pray a little harder. Read a little more.* Those things had worked for me in the past.

147

But they weren't working now.

Things got so bad that I realized I needed to see a counselor before I broke. In that first meeting with the counselor, he asked a question I wasn't expecting. "Jeff, when was the last time you played?"

*Huh? Play?* I didn't say it out loud, but I was thinking, *What do you mean? Like with blocks and toy cars? That would be like twenty years ago, sir.*

After it became clear I didn't have an answer for him, he said something I'll never forget. "Jeff, play is the oxygen for your entire being and soul and day. If you don't play, you will die— emotionally at least. Is that what you want?"

He went on to say that no one wants to follow a man who doesn't play. Men who don't play become rigid, grumpy, short-fused, and exhausted—and they spread that vibe to everyone around them.

An epiphany washed over me. He was right. The reason I felt burned out was because I *was*. The reason I felt dead was because I *was*. He'd nailed the diagnosis. I did not have a consistent habit of any activity that made my soul come alive. I didn't have time. In fact, I'd become convinced that pursuing such things was self-ish and wasteful with how busy my life was.

Before I go any further, let's define some terms and clar-ify what my counselor meant, because as I dove headfirst into this topic, my first mistake was the same one you are probably making right now as you read this. When I say *play*, don't think frivolousness. I'm going to let Dr. Stuart Brown and Christopher Vaughan, authorities on the psychological and emotional benefits of play, provide some insight:

Play is the state of mind that one has when absorbed in an activity that provides enjoyment and a suspension of sense of time. And play is self-motivated so you want to do it again and again . . . The characteristics of play all have to do with motivation and mental attitude, not with . . . the behavior itself. Two people might be throwing a ball . . . or typing words on a computer, and one might be playing while the other is not. To tell which one is playing . . . you have to infer from their expressions and the details of their actions.[7]

Play isn't just about having fun; it is a deeply necessary biological response for our growth, learning, and development. Without play we never risk or explore. We freeze in our state of fear or stress. A study with rats on the concept of play supported this point. Researchers divided the rats into two groups. For one group they fostered and encouraged play when they were young, but for the second group they prohibited play. I didn't know this, but rats are very playful in their early years, constantly exploring, wrestling, squeaking—playing. But for that second group of rats, the researchers shut down the playful behavior every time it started. When the rats reached adulthood, the researchers put each group in a car filled with cat pheromones.

The initial response was identical. All the rats immediately ran and hid, burrowing somewhere in the car they hoped would be safe. But what happened next is shocking. The rats who never were allowed to play

**Play isn't just about having fun; it is a deeply necessary biological response for our growth, learning, and development.**

didn't move again. After initially scurrying into a hiding place, they stayed there, frozen in fear, and died. But the other group? Slowly but surely, they came back out, sniffed around, checked out the scene, and determined they were safe, despite the alarming scent of the cat pheromones.[8]

The takeaway? In the animal kingdom, play promotes a healthier vision of risk balanced against other needs. Play lays the foundation for exploration and a massive sense of curiosity. It keeps you soft, curious, and nimble. But a lack of play leads to crippling anxiety, fear, and failure in the face of challenges.

Do the words *soft*, *curious*, *nimble*, and *playful* describe you?

They weren't words that described me.

And despite having a life packed with activities that should have been providing me with a powerful sense of purpose and filling my soul with meaning, I was instead drifting further into the shadow of futility.

Do you want to be remembered? Do you want a legacy? Be a man who radiates joy, play, strength, and a smile when others are in your orbit. That will change lives. Beyond learning to rule your passions, finding your calling and assignment, and living by a code so that you are always ready for your kairos moment—make sure you carve out time for play. As you hold all these things in balance, the bright light of purpose, meaning, and joy will send the shadow of futility far away from your heart.

# THE SHADOW OF APATHY

*The Lie:* There is nothing worth giving yourself for.

*The Truth:* You were born to live a life of consequence.

*War must be, while we defend our lives against a destroyer who would devour all; but I do not love the bright sword for its sharpness, nor the arrow for its swiftness, nor the warrior for his glory. I love only that which they defend.*

**—J. R. R. TOLKIEN**

*Never be lacking in zeal, but keep your spiritual fervor, serving the Lord.*

**—ROMANS 12:11**

**We recently surveyed four hundred women,** asking what they believe is wrong with men in the modern world. The answers were fascinating, but one theme seemed to stand out from the replies we received.

Can you guess what it was?

*Apathy.*

Without vision, people perish (Proverbs 29:18). Without vision, men get stuck. It seems to the watching world that the hearts of a generation of men are perishing. Many men feel there is nothing worth rousing themselves for. To quote the prophet Tyler Durden, "We are the middle children of history, raised by television to believe that someday we'll be millionaires and movie stars and rock stars, but we won't. And we're just learning this fact."[1]

Men seem like they are stuck, paralyzed, drifting through life on autopilot. The feedback from the surveys was brutal:

Men today lack purpose and drive.
Men today lack direction in life.
Men today lack initiative in relationships.
Men today lack a sense of vocational call.

Lack, lack, lack, lack, lack. No initiative, no direction, no drive. The shadow of apathy is standing over a generation of men.

## THE MALE MALAISE

These days, the mere suggestion that men are struggling is often met with strong emotional pushback.

"The patriarchy is still in control!"

"Societal structures were built by and for men, and they're still reaping the benefits!"

"The gender pay gap still exists!"

And there is some truth and validity to these claims. Women have historically been dismissed, marginalized, or excluded from a male-dominated world. Harsh and restrictive gender roles have robbed women of agency, dignity, and fuller cultural expression. We, the authors of this book, are committed to the empowerment and equality of women in the world. And we agree there is still much work to do.

Yes, there are a few rich men at the top of the food chain, ruling with a kind of influence and power that kings of another generation would envy. But they are not representative of most men. Many men today feel enveloped in an apathetic haze.

**Many men today feel enveloped in an apathetic haze.**

In an article in the *Atlantic* entitled "Colleges Have a Guy Problem," Derek Thompson highlighted this cultural reality for men:

> The sociologist Kathryn Edin has written that men without college degrees in deindustrialized America have been adrift for decades. They face the simultaneous shocks of lost jobs, disintegrating nuclear families, and rising deaths of despair in their communities. As 20th-century institutions have crumbled around them, these men have withdrawn from organized religion. Their marriage rates have fallen in lockstep with their church attendance. Far from the ordered progression of the mid-century American archetype—marriage, career, house, and yard—men without college degrees are more likely to live what Edin and other researchers call "haphazard" lives, detached from family, faith, and work.[2]

*Haphazard* and *detached*—these two words describe so many men we meet today. I don't think men see these changes as liberation from traditional masculine roles, or a chance to party a bit more during extended adolescence. Most experience this like the loss of a pathway to a meaningful life. The changing world is making it hard for men to figure out how to build meaningful lives. Men today deeply struggle to find direction and connection.

I (Jon) have been a pastor of a church in the middle of New York City for nearly twenty years. During that time, I have repeatedly heard women lament the lack of godly men in the church. Most pastors I talk to today say the same thing. Congregations are filled with wonderful, mature, and thoughtful women, who cannot for the life of them seem to find their equal among the men. It's not that they need a man to be successful—most of them already are. Rather, they are seeking companionship from those whose maturity and vision track with their own.

Where are all the men? Stuck in the masculine malaise.

I remember a young man in our community who started dating a fantastic woman he really liked. They had similar interests, a shared cultural background, and commitment to their faith. But after only a few months they broke up. "What happened?" I asked, surprised because of how much he liked her.

"I felt like I couldn't live up," he said. "She made more money than me, had a better career trajectory, and went to a better graduate school. I didn't want to deal with the cynicism of her family about my history or success in life." Call him insecure or immature or whatever you want, but the shame and sense of failure is real for so many. They open the door for apathy to come in.

I don't know about you, but when I hear stories like this, a deep sadness settles in.

The movement of Jesus is called to be a movement of visionaries. It's meant to be a movement of young men seeing visions and old men dreaming dreams (Acts 2:17). It's meant to be a movement of the Spirit being poured out, eyes being opened, hunger being restored. It's meant to be a movement that calls men to something beyond themselves. It's a movement that turned fishermen into apostles and sinners into martyrs. It's a movement that draws men out of their self-absorbed lives and into the cause of Jesus in their time.

## AN INVITATION IN A TIME OF DECLINE

When we read the New Testament, we may be tempted to think that the men in the Bible struggled with different issues than we do. But although the cultural situations are different, the core issues are the same, and that's why 1 and 2 Timothy are some of my favorite books in the Bible. Timothy seemed to be struggling with issues very similar to ours.

Timothy was living in a city dominated by the worship of the goddess Artemis. The religious practices related to Artemis exerted control over the economy, cultural institutions, and calendar. Timothy was leading a church in the middle of that city with a series of overwhelming problems. The glory days of ministry were behind him. The miracles were gone, Paul had left, the wonder was done. Heretical teachers, domineering women, fighting men, a lack of leadership, conflict between the rich and the poor, people being led astray—he was facing it all.

Timothy was sincere, but he was struggling. He had some health issues. He was neglecting his gift, and the flame had gone out. Timothy had forgotten the prophetic promises spoken over his life that enabled him to fight. Timothy was shrinking back because he was young, and he needed hope. He needed a crew to run with. Paul knew Timothy wouldn't break out of this malaise alone, so he wrote to Timothy seeking to strengthen his heart:

"Join with me in suffering, like a good soldier of Christ Jesus. No one serving as a soldier gets entangled in civilian affairs, but rather tries to please his commanding officer" (2 Timothy 2:3–4).

If Paul were writing to young men in the church today, he would echo many of these same concerns. He would call us to rise above the apathy and overwhelm of the moment. He would remind us of the vision and calling we have.

> In a time of decline, it is more important than ever that men form these bands of brothers.

Do you have men who speak these sorts of things over your life? Who can walk with you through the suffering? Who reminds you of your calling? Are you that kind of presence in the lives of other men? In a time of decline, it is more important than ever that men form these bands of brothers. We cannot stay the course alone.

## A GOD AT WAR

How a man views God makes all the difference in the world for how he practices his faith. His view of God determines his view of himself. The metaphors used to describe God are wide and varied in the Bible, but not so much in the modern church. We have seemed to fixate on a few to the neglect of others.

We all know about God as a shepherd. We love Psalm 23, with its poetic language and the promise of guidance and care. Maybe we don't spend as much time thinking about how the metaphor makes us sheep, but it is comforting and familiar, even if a touch distant from how we live today.

We all know about God as a gardener. The metaphor of vineyards, pruning, and abiding are also widely used. Ever been to Napa Valley? Pure magic. Who doesn't love the idea of seasons, the slow bearing of fruit, and all things being made beautiful in their time?

We all know about God as father. It was Jesus' favorite word for God. We all ache to belong, to have a family, a spirit that cries abba. No one wants an orphan spirit. Some people today love this metaphor, calling God "Papa" or "Daddy" when they pray.

But there is another view of God, one that is overlooked and confronts the spirit of apathy so many men face. God is a general. He is mighty in battle and skilled in war. Yes, you are a sheep; yes, you are a branch; yes, you are a child; but you are also a soldier. You are in a fight.

Psalm 24:8 reminds us about this aspect of the God we serve:

> Who is this King of glory?
> > The LORD strong and mighty,
> > the LORD mighty in battle.

After the Israelites triumphed over the Egyptians, they broke out in song, singing,

> The LORD is a warrior;
> > the LORD is his name.

**(EXODUS 15:3)**

Isaiah 42:13 tells us,

> The LORD will go out like a warrior,
> He will stir His zeal like a man of war.
> He will shout, indeed, He will raise a war cry. (NASB)

The God you serve isn't just pruning and guiding and hugging; the God you serve is at war.

## LIVING ON A BATTLEFIELD

The context of our faith determines how we live that faith. If we see ourselves in a garden, we live one way. If we see ourselves on a battlefield, we live another way. We must not confuse our original design (Eden) and ultimate destination (new creation) with our current reality. We are in the middle of the story, and it is a war. It's a fight between good and evil, justice and injustice, liberation and oppression, God and Satan. We are in a war, and the battle is for our hearts.

**We are in a war, and the battle is for our hearts.**

I (Jon) am amazed at how naive believers can be today. I am amazed how distorted our faith has become. I am going to share a modern version of the gospel, one you would hear in the majority of conservative churches. But I have left something out. See if you can notice what it is.

In the beginning God created the world. He made humanity as his image bearers to love and serve him. They chose

THE SHADOW OF APATHY

to rebel, desiring to determine what was good and evil for themselves. This sin resulted in their expulsion from Eden and the entrance of sin into the world. The result of this sin was separation from God and physical and spiritual death. In his grace God worked a plan of salvation into the human story, first through the formation of the people of Israel, then through sending his Son, Jesus. Christ came and lived a perfect life, died for our sin on the cross, and rose again on the third day. If we repent of our sin, and trust in his finished work, we can become children of God. We are given a new identity and a calling to seek his kingdom and walk with him in this life. When we die we will live forever in a new heaven and earth when God comes to restore all things.

Sounds pretty good, doesn't it? Maybe even a bit more robust than the typical sinner's prayer. But did you notice what was missing?

It wasn't extra narrative details.

It wasn't a mention of the old covenant.

It wasn't the miracles.

*It was Satan.*

We have taken the Enemy out of our story.

If you don't have Satan in your story, you will turn others into Satan.

If you don't have demons in your story, you will demonize others.

So much of what is wrong with our modern faith is that we have mapped spiritual elements onto human elements. Paul said we don't wrestle against flesh and blood. Tell that to the Western church.

## THE ENEMY

Behind the cultural and sociological dynamics affecting men today are larger spiritual ones. We have an enemy who hates men. You have an enemy who hates you. Jesus said, "The thief comes only to steal and kill and destroy" (John 10:10). You have to take that seriously. He wants to steal your vision and dreams. He wants to kill your integrity and relationships. He wants to destroy your future and your hope. He wants to delude you into thinking there is no place for you to thrive in the world today. But it's all a lie.

I (Jon) have a friend who was perpetually caught up in a cycle of shame. He had a serious porn addiction and was constantly sabotaging his close relationships due to fear and shame. It went on like this for years. Then one day he showed up at our group and everything seemed different. I made a point of asking him what happened that had caused his countenance to change.

"It's really kind of simple," he said. "I saw myself in a new light. Here I was sitting alone in a dark room. I was masturbating looking at violent porn. I was isolated, living in a fantasy world, and hating myself. And I had a realization. *This isn't who I am. This isn't even what I want. I'm not living my plan for my life, let alone God's. This is what Satan wants. He wants me separated from those I love, commodifying women, crippled by shame, and shrinking back in guilt.*

It's not that I don't still struggle at all; it's just that my life has been reframed. I am not a pawn in Satan's plan; I'm seeking God's call for my life. I'm living in a different story now."[3]

When you start hating sin, you stop hating yourself. When you start hating Satan, you stop hating your life. That's why the apostle Peter reminded us, "Be alert and of sober mind. Your enemy the devil prowls around like a roaring lion looking for someone to devour. Resist him, standing firm in the faith" (1 Peter 5:8–9).

Don't be naive. Pay attention. Resist. Resist the passivity that says you do not matter. Resist the shame that says you are your mistakes. Resist the lie that you will never change. Stand firm and hold your ground. Remember your identity and calling. Show up with a humble defiance.

## A SOLDIER OF CHRIST

Paul invited Timothy to join with him in suffering, like a good soldier of Christ Jesus. He invited you to do the same.

We are all familiar with the military today. You may have even served in the military. It's obvious that when you join the military your lifestyle changes. You can't live like everyone else. You can't go where everyone else goes. You can't think like everyone else.

It was no different in the Roman world. When you enlisted in the Roman army, you had your name officially registered with the military, severing you from civilian life. You had to swear an oath of allegiance to Rome, building a bond of allegiance to the empire. And you got a tattoo, a visible mark that identified you with your legion. You couldn't marry, and you served your brothers for roughly twenty years. Any mutiny or abandonment was punishable by death. Your vision became clearer, your relationships more defined, your life more disciplined.

Satan hates men with vision. He hates men who refuse the mediocrity of their day. He hates men with an insurgent mentality. He will do anything within his power to sabotage their call. Sometimes he uses a direct assault, tempting us with what we know is obviously wrong. But he knows the best way to immobilize a man is more subtle. His most effective strategy to destroy men is to lull them to sleep with apathy—to ease them into a sense that there is nothing to do, nothing to become, nothing to fight—to get them to sip the sweet wine of self-pity and despair and never realize their strength.

C. S. Lewis articulated this strategy in his book *The Screwtape Letters*:

> It does not matter how small the sins are provided that their cumulative effect is to edge the man away from the Light and out into the Nothing. Murder is no better than cards if cards can do the trick. Indeed the safest road to Hell is the gradual one—the gentle slope, soft underfoot, without sudden turnings, without milestones, without signposts.[4]

Away from the light and into the nothing—this is Satan's plan for you, for you to slip into your shadow calling.

## THE SHADOW CALLING: CIVILIAN AFFAIRS

If Satan can't destroy your faith, he will try to get you to settle for a shadow version of it. He will attempt to seduce you out of the war into civilian affairs. Paul warned Timothy against this: "No one serving as a soldier gets entangled in civilian affairs" (2 Timothy 2:4).

One of the most grievous sins in the military is for a man to abandon his post. Imagine a soldier going to a movie in the middle of a firefight. Imagine a man going to Walmart in the middle of a war.

To be clear, Paul was not warning Timothy against things that are sinful. He was warning him against things that are stupid. These things might not have been bad in themselves. They were just inappropriate for the calling. That's why Paul reminded the Corinthians, "'You have the right to do anything,' you say—but not everything is beneficial. 'I have the right to do anything'—but not everything is constructive. No one should seek their own good, but the good of others" (1 Corinthians 10:23–24).

*Entangled* is an interesting word. In 2 Timothy 2:4, Paul used a passive form of *emplekó*, which means "to weave." We take these small things, these innocent things, and we weave them into our schedules. We weave them into our imaginations, we weave them through our resources, and the next thing we know, we are caught up and can't break free.

## ENTANGLED IN THE TRIVIAL

So many men get caught up in civilian affairs today, in trivial things that rob them of their passion. Jane McGonigal pointed out that "the average young person racks up 10,000 hours of gaming by the age of 21. That's almost exactly as much time as they spend in a classroom during all of middle school and high school if they have perfect attendance. Most astonishingly, 5 million gamers in the U.S. are spending more than 40 hours a week playing games—the same as a full-time job!"[5]

It's not that this is sinful, it's just that it's poor stewardship. If a man redirected that time toward other ends, his life would be immeasurably better.

## ONE HUNDRED HOURS

We may sound harsh here, or even a touch legalistic. But there is no finger-pointing going on, just an honest acknowledgment of how easy it is for a man to get caught up in lesser things. I (Jon) started watching a show about a fictional family that owned a ranch in Montana. I had COVID-19, which was my excuse for diving in. I was not prepared for how deep into the series I would get. I started doing research on the history of Montana, whether or not you could rent the house it was filmed in for family vacations, and how much value a seminary degree would have when I changed careers to become a cowboy. Then there was the issue of the spin-off shows. It turned out the wormhole was quite deep. Apparently, other years in the family's history were worth diving into also—1883, 1923 . . . so many good years to show on television. I found my mind and heart getting drawn into an imaginary and godless world.

When it was all said and done, I had invested more than one hundred hours into fictional ranching in Montana. One hundred hours may not seem like much, but you can get a lot done in that

THE SHADOW OF APATHY

amount of time. I started to do some one-hundred-hour experiments with things that were more redemptive.

It turns out you can write a book in one hundred hours.

You can teach your son to drive a car in one hundred hours.

You can do every single chore your wife has been reminding you about for years in *less than* one hundred hours!

I would give anything to have another one hundred hours with my kids now that I am an empty nester.

In a world like ours, spiritual warfare might be as simple as canceling your Netflix subscription or turning off *Fortnite*. We must be willing to do whatever it takes—because when you are in a war, a distracted man is a man at risk.

. . .

On May 26, 2018, Mamoudou Gassama, a Malian immigrant, was walking through a neighborhood in northern Paris, headed to watch the Champions League game between Real Madrid and Liverpool on TV. As he walked along the Rue Marx-Dormoy, he saw a crowd had gathered and was anxiously looking up at an apartment building. A small boy was dangling from the edge of a fourth-floor balcony, at times hanging by one hand. A neighbor was desperately trying to reach the child over a partition to bring him to safety.

The twenty-two-year-old Gassama didn't hesitate. He climbed the four floors in thirty seconds, and then carried the child to safety. Dubbed "the French Spiderman," he was granted citizenship and seen as a national hero. But questions began to emerge about how the child got there in the first place. Where were the parents? What had gone wrong? Reporters revealed "the boy's father was not at home at all, and that he had left his son alone to go shopping. The father delayed his return so he could play Pokemon Go."[6] A grown man went shopping and stopped to play a video game while his son was fighting for his life. It turns out that getting entangled in civilian affairs can have consequences.

We live in an age of radical individualism. It's an age that continually urges us to focus on ourselves. Our desires and wounds can have a kind of gravitational pull that causes us to collapse back in on ourselves. Selfishness reduces a man's vision. It causes him to lose sight of anything beyond himself. It pulls him out of the fight and into his head.

Jeff Cook wrote, "The more I make my life, my well-being, my enlightenment, and my success primary, the farther I step from reality. Thus, the hell-bound do not travel downward; they travel inward, cocooning themselves behind a mass of vanity, personal rights, religiosity, and defensiveness. Obsession with self is the defining mark of a disintegrating soul."[7]

You are not a civilian; you are a soldier. You are not in a fairy tale; you are in a fight. Your time matters, your vision matters, you matter. Your life is worth more than you know.

## THE MISALLOCATION OF A MAN'S STRENGTH

Proverbs 31 is probably the most famous chapter about women in the Bible. "A wife of noble character who can find?" (v. 10). But in our pursuit of the perfect wife, many have forgotten how the chapter starts: "Do not spend your strength on women, your vigor on those who ruin kings" (v. 3).

This is an ancient warning, but it still applies for modern men.

Scholars believe this passage is referring to King Solomon, a man granted more wisdom than any man in history, who stewarded it more poorly than any man in history. Toward the end of his life, Solomon got distracted. His distraction led to disobedience.

First Kings 11:1–8 shares this in heartbreaking detail:

King Solomon, however, loved many foreign women besides Pharaoh's daughter—Moabites, Ammonites, Edomites, Sidonians and Hittites. They were from nations about which the LORD had told the Israelites, "You must not intermarry with them, because they will surely turn your hearts after their gods." Nevertheless, Solomon held fast to them in love. He had seven hundred wives of royal birth and three hundred concubines, and his wives led him astray. As Solomon grew old, his wives turned his heart after other gods, and his heart was not fully devoted to the LORD his God, as the heart of David his father had been. He followed Ashtoreth the goddess of the Sidonians, and Molek the detestable god of the Ammonites. . . . On a hill east of Jerusalem, Solomon built a high place for Chemosh the detestable god of Moab, and for Molek the detestable god of the Ammonites. He did the same for all his foreign wives, who burned incense and offered sacrifices to their gods.

Solomon took the resources he was given to serve his people and squandered them on idolatry. He gave his strength to women instead of the people God had called him to serve. His vigor, a man's distinctive gift, was wasted on building shrines to other gods.

When a man gives his strength to lesser things, everyone suffers. When a man wastes his vigor, entitlement and complacency set in. God gives men strength for a reason.

Look at what verses 4 through 9 of Proverbs 31 say:

It is not for kings, Lemuel—it is not for kings to drink wine, not for rulers to crave beer, lest they drink and forget what has been decreed, and deprive all the oppressed of their rights. . . . Speak up for those who cannot speak for themselves, for the rights of all who are destitute. Speak up and judge fairly; defend the rights of the poor and needy.

God gives men strength to serve others. We are called to use it to speak up for the poor. We are to use it to confront evil, to fight injustice, to be men for others. As the saying goes, "The only thing necessary for the triumph of evil is for good men to do nothing."[8]

Now with all this talk about war, generals, soldiers, and civilians, you may be nervous about such militant language propping up stereotypes, culture wars, and clichés. In no way are we glorifying violence or aggression for its own sake or promoting John Wayne kinds of stereotypes. Strength can manifest itself through a myriad of personalities. It can show up in quiet resolve. It can show up in faithful presence. It can show up in perseverance. It can show up with patience and kindness. It can show up in resilience through suffering.

But ultimately, we fight because we love. We are compelled to act for the good of others. We are compelled to move because we can't sit by and watch others suffer. We are compelled because we are empathetically connected to the struggles of others. We fight because evil does not give up on its own. We fight because there is so much at stake.

In 1912, General William Booth, founder of the Salvation Army, entered Royal Albert Hall in London to a packed crowd of seven thousand Salvationists to give his last, most notable address. Booth's words summed up his own sixty-year ministry and the ministry we are called to as followers of Jesus:

> While women weep, as they do now, I'll fight; while children go hungry, as they do now, I'll fight; while men go to prison, in and out, in and out, as they do now, I'll fight; while there is a poor lost girl upon the streets, while there remains one dark soul without the light of God, I'll fight, I'll fight to the very end![9]

## GENTLE JESUS, MEEK AND VIOLENT

We all want to follow Jesus well. We want to steward our strength properly, break the spirit of apathy, and live for the purposes of God in our day. But the balance is tricky. It's hard to be aggressive *and* kind. It's hard to hate evil *and* love the people who commit it. I (Jon) was wrestling with things when I came across a talk that held them together in a biblical balance. One phrase from that talk has stood out to me ever since: "Be violent with the spirit, but gentle with the person."[10]

The pastor was explaining the need to use our spiritual authority to engage in warfare, but to be merciful and kind to the people caught up in it. This tension helps us make sense of how Jesus did his ministry. Jesus got angry, turned over tables, cleansed the temple, cast out demons, and announced judgment on a city; yet he did it with tears, honored individual dignity, and made space for personal restoration.

Jesus was both violent and gentle.

When Jesus encountered demonized people, there was often a violent confrontation. When forced to leave, the demons shrieked, shook, and often left people looking as though they were dead. Jesus rebuked them, cast them out, and enforced the kingdom of God. Yet, he was always kind to those possessed by demons.

He delivered the boy his disciples couldn't and gave him back to his father (Matthew 17:14–21).

He delivered the demoniac, then restored him spiritually, physically, emotionally, and socially (Luke 8:26–39). He treated him with dignity and kindness.

He cast seven demons out of Mary Magdalene (Luke 8:2), then included her as one of his key disciples, appearing to her after the resurrection and entrusting her as a witness (John 20:11–18).

These are examples of the violent spiritual warfare and the personal kindness of Jesus.

**Jesus was both violent and gentle.**

When Peter was filled with worldly ambition, Jesus rebuked him in the strongest possible terms: "Get behind me, Satan!" (Matthew 16:23). Yet, Jesus was so gentle with Peter, forgiving him for his denial, finding him when he went fishing, and restoring his calling (John 21:15–17). Jesus raged against the corruption and hypocrisy of the religious leaders. He called them sons of hell, whitewashed tombs, and blind guides. Yet, he made space for Nicodemus, which resulted in his becoming a disciple. He condemned the system but was kind to the man.

We are called to fight. Romans 12:9 tells us to "hate what is evil; cling to what is good." Passivity and toleration are not the way of the kingdom or the ministry model of Jesus. Yet we must remember who and what we are fighting. We are called to contend for the truth, but to do it with love. Men, you are called to be like Jesus in this way. You are called to have a combination of gentleness and violence, but it must be deployed properly. Paul wrote:

> For though we live in the world, we do not wage war as the world does. The weapons we fight with are not the weapons of the world. On the contrary, they have divine power to demolish strongholds. We demolish arguments and every pretension that sets itself up against the knowledge of God, and we take captive every thought to make it obedient to Christ. (2 Corinthians 10:3–5)

Make sure you are involved in spiritual warfare, not just cultural warfare.

Make sure your weapons are spiritual, not just political.

Make sure you are relying on God's power, not human power.

Make sure you are tearing down strongholds, not people.

Fight the right way, in the right war.

### Be Violent with the Spirit

Rage against the spirit of mammon that creates poverty without care and leads people away from God.

Be violent against the spirit of lust that commodifies sexuality and dehumanizes others.

Be violent against the spirit of indifference that lets others suffer while we walk by.

Be violent against the spirit of tyranny that oppresses others and exerts the self.

## Be Gentle with People

Be merciful to those who doubt.

Do not condemn people caught in sin.

Weep over the shepherdless masses.

Love your enemy and do good to those who persecute you.

As Paul wrote to Timothy, "Gently instruct those who oppose the truth. Perhaps God will change those people's hearts, and they will learn the truth. Then they will come to their senses and escape from the devil's trap. For they have been held captive by him to do whatever he wants" (2 Timothy 2:25–26 NLT).

We need men who are both gentle and violent, men who can hate and love at the same time, men who can both weep and go to war.

And remember, in Jesus you don't lack a thing. You have everything you need for life and godliness (2 Peter 1:3). You are seated with Christ in the heavenly realms (Ephesians 2:6). There are good works prepared in advance for you to walk in (Ephesians 2:10). Reject apathy. Free yourself from civilian affairs. Level up. It's time for you to reenlist.

That's how you will please your commanding officer.

# CONCLUSION AND CALL

Becoming Light

He who follows Me shall not walk in darkness, but
have the light of life.

**—JESUS (JOHN 8:12 NKJV)**

*"Wake up, sleeper,*
*rise from the dead,*
*and Christ will shine on you."*

**—PAUL TO THE EPHESIANS (5:14)**

**You have been on a real journey reading this book,** and we want to take a moment to honor you for making it this far. Plenty of men don't finish books. Many more never get below the surface of their lives. So we want to celebrate your effort and determination to be a man of depth in a shallow world.

So many men today never reach their redemptive potential. They don't take the journey to the end. They sit in church and sing the songs and say amen without ever really confronting the forces killing their hearts. They stop fighting the shadows and start accepting them. They get numb, settle, or collapse inward to medicate their quiet desperation. So being willing to examine the forces coming against you and resist them is something you should be proud of. And you are going to need grace to keep pushing forward, because the more you grow, the stronger the resistance will get.

The psychiatrist Carl Jung said, "One does not become enlightened by imagining figures of light, but by making the darkness conscious."[1] So many Christian men today think that if we just imagine things differently, we will become better men. But the power of positive thinking hasn't worked. So much of what men have been told is nothing more than simply "imagining light." You can't imagine your way into manhood; you have to be made into a man. As a result, so many are sabotaged by shadow forces they are not even aware of. Hearing from Jung again, "Until you make the unconscious conscious, it will direct your life and you will call it fate."[2]

So many men allow these shadow forces to direct their lives. They are run by a shadow government they cannot name, hindered by a shadow calling they didn't choose, and blocked from seeing all God has for them. Then they never see the glory of God and the glorious future he has for them. This is what the Enemy wants—for you to stop trusting, start striving, and manage your anxiety and disappointment until you die.

But this is not your fate.

You have been willing to take what's been hiding in the shadows of your life and examine it. You have dragged out what's lurking in the darkness and called it to account. You have learned to see past the strategy of the Enemy to keep you from the grace of God and the future he has for you.

You have learned to

- fight the shadow of despair with hope,
- fight the shadow of loneliness with community,
- fight the shadow of shame with vulnerability,

- fight the shadow of lust with faithfulness,
- fight the shadow of ambition with a kingdom vision,
- fight the shadow of futility with calling, and
- fight the shadow of apathy with a cause.

## FIGHT THE ENEMIES OF LIFE

But as you move forward into the light, you must not get complacent.

James Hollis noted that every morning there are two forces that stand over a man's life to stop him from making progress.[3] They appear every day and threaten and intimidate us. He called them the enemies of life. These enemies are fear and lethargy.

Fear tells us . . .

You are not going to be able to do this.

You are not going to be able to sustain this over time.

You are going to shrink back into your old habits.

People will reject you.

Others will think you are self-righteous.

Women will not understand you.

Some of this may be true, but none of that really matters because it is the affirmation of heaven that counts, not the acceptance of the world. The "well done" of the Father will drown out the clamor of the world. Do not let your enemy intimidate you back into the shadows.

Satan's main plan for your life will be intimidation and fear.

> The "well done" of the Father will drown out the clamor of the world.

And he can be good at it. Fear can roll in like a fog that blocks our vision and ability to move forward. It can paralyze us from acting and heading into the fight. But the substance of what we fear is much less than the idea of fear. I once heard that a fog that is one hundred feet deep and covers seven city blocks when reduced to its essence would barely fill a cup of water. But spread out into 60 billion droplets it can have a devastating effect.

Jesus' number one promise to us is that as we walk as men in the world, he will be with us always (Matthew 28:20). Hebrews 13:6 says, "So we say with confidence, 'The Lord is my helper; I will not be afraid. What can mere mortals do to me?'" And Jesus reminds us that if we fear God, we don't have to fear anything else.

Do not be afraid of Satan bringing your past up against you; you have been delivered from the kingdom of darkness and transferred into the kingdom of light.

Do not be afraid of discouragement and despair; Jesus will meet you there and walk with you into the dawn.

Do not be afraid of what the culture thinks about you; you do not need the feeble applause of the fickle crowd.

It's amazing how light removes fear. When you are in a dark alley or the woods or your own backyard late at night, your mind can play tricks on you, intimidating you with the unknown. But when you turn on a light or shine a flashlight, you see clearly to confront what's there.

You are a man of the light. Fear not. Move through shadows with confidence.

The second enemy of life is lethargy. "Lethargy is defined as "a lack of energy or vigor; sluggishness. A lack of interest or enthusiasm; apathy."

Lethargy tells us . . .

You don't have to do this now. You can do it later.
Stop being so intense.
You probably won't make a difference anyway.
You are not missing out on that much anyway.
Mediocrity is safe; risk isn't worth it.

. . .

In Greek mythology, one of the five rivers of Hades was called Lethe. Drinking from it made people forget. It led people into a kind of mindless oblivion. This is one of the great traps for men in the world, sipping from the river of lethargy. You lose your urgency and passion when you drink of the trivial and the trite. A man's potential can slowly die while he amuses himself to death. Refuse to go out like this. The story you are in is a story of awakening. It is a story of being called out of your sleep. Let these words seep into your soul:

- "Wake up, sleeper, rise from the dead, and Christ will shine on you," Paul charged the Ephesians (Ephesians 5:14).
- "Wake up! Strengthen what remains and is about to die, for I have found your deeds unfinished in the sight of my God," Jesus said to the Church in Sardis (Revelation 3:2).
- "The hour has already come for you to wake up from your

slumber, because our salvation is nearer now than when we first believed. The night is nearly over; the day is almost here," Paul urged the church in Rome (Romans 13:11–12).

- "You are all children of the light and children of the day. We do not belong to the night or to the darkness. So then, let us not be like others, who are asleep, but let us be awake and sober. For those who sleep, sleep at night, and those who get drunk, get drunk at night. But since we belong to the day, let us be sober," Paul exhorted the Thessalonians (1 Thessalonians 5:5–8).

## REFUSE TO EXCHANGE SUSTAINABILITY FOR MEDIOCRITY

One of the most consistent pieces of feedback you will hear as you start to move forward is that you need to "calm down." The last few years have been hard for us all, and burnout is at an all-time high, but among the legitimate struggles and concerns, something else has snuck in—a kind of selfish preservation. I don't want you to trade burning out for not burning at all. I don't want you to swap sustainability for mediocrity.

When he was in his sixties, Nobel- and Pulitzer Prize–winning author John Steinbeck set out on a road trip around America to see what had become of the country he loved. He wasn't seeking to recapture his youth or revisit the glory days; he simply wanted to push into what was stirring in his heart. He had a desire to find his place in a changing nation and rekindle the sense of adventure that grows dull in the hearts of men his age.

And then the concerns began to roll in. Many thought the trip was too much, unnecessary, and a threat to his life. It was going to be a very large undertaking of resources and energy. Why couldn't he settle down with some smaller hobbies and a few luxuries? He had earned—even deserved—the opportunity to relax. He had nothing left to prove. The voice of late-life lethargy began to speak.

His reply to these concerns was profound. In *Travels with Charley*, the book documenting the trip, he wrote:

> It happens to many men, and I think doctors have memorized the litany. It had happened to so many of my friends. The lecture ends, "Slow down. You're not as young as you once were." I had seen so many begin to pack their lives in cotton wool, smother their impulses, hood their passions, and gradually retire from their manhood into a kind of spiritual and physical semi-invalidism. In this they are encouraged by wives and relatives, and it's such a sweet trap. Who doesn't like to be a center for concern? A kind of second childhood falls on so many men. They trade their violence for the promise of a small increase of life span. In effect, the head of the house becomes the youngest child.[4]

Do not retire from manhood. Do not fall back into a second childhood.

I am not for foolhardy bravado, but the sweet trap must be resisted. Hebrews 11 is called the hall of faith, not the hall of sustainability. You must press into the call of God on your life. He calls you to live from your heart. He wants you to step into the unknown, the place of risk and faith. That can be as small as joining a new community of men or as large as changing your career. You can't let everyone's concern for you drown out God's call on your life. Listen to his voice. It will be the one that calls you out of comfort, calls you to the cross, and calls you to find your life by losing it.

Steinbeck went on: "And I have searched for this possibility with a kind of horror. . . . I did not want to surrender fierceness for a small gain in yardage. My wife married a man; I saw no reason why she should inherit a baby."[5]

Whew.

*My wife married a man; I saw no reason why she should inherit a baby.*

What sort of men is our world inheriting today? How much fierceness have we surrendered for yardage? To get this right you are going to need to prioritize your calling, not just the voices of concern. Only you and the Holy Spirit truly know if you are living your call with all your heart, and if the gifts of God are aflame within. Resist the sweet drink of lethargy. Spit out the halfhearted life.

## BECOME A MAN THE WORLD NEEDS

It's the middle of the day in ancient Greece and the sun is shining in all its fullness.

A strange man appears walking through the center of the city carrying a lamp burning at full brightness. Slowly everyone turns to look at this bizarre sight. A man in the middle of the day carrying a lamp as though it's night.

It is our old friend, Diogenes, the man who told Alexander the Great to step out of his light.

"What are you doing, Diogenes?" one man asks.

"I am looking for a man," Diogenes replies.[6]

Looking for a man?

Why the lamp? Where was he trying to find one? What message was he trying to send?

Diogenes lived at a time when society was putting forth its ideas of the kind of men it needed—the virtuous man, the contemplative man, the glorious man. Yet he was frustrated with the answers that were given in his day. Men were superficial. Men defined themselves by the wrong things. Men were addicted to status and reputation, and they were slaves to the trite and the vicious.

Diogenes was saying, "I am looking for a man and cannot find any in the cultural options."

In some sense this is the journey you have been on in reading this book. In your heart you know that God has called you to become a man in full, but the cultural options don't fit who you are meant to be.

You can't let *ideology* define your view of manhood. We know in our hearts that we can't just declare ourselves to be men simply because we choose to identify as one. Masculinity doesn't work that way.

And you can't reduce your vision of manhood to *biology*. An "adult human male" may tell you something about how a man's body has developed, but it can't tell you how his heart and soul have developed. Biology is important but insufficient to give you clarity to move forward.[7]

And you can't let *stereotypes* be your guide. Some of the strongest and bravest men I know don't manifest the traits of strength and courage in stereotypical ways.[8]

And we know that we can't let the *culture* dictate our vision or we will be driven by emotions and impulses. Men who are controlled by these kinds of impulses have done so much damage in our world today.

We need men who are defined by a biblical vision of manhood. We need men who see themselves as image bearers and sons of God—those entrusted with power and responsibility to create, cultivate, care, and defend our world for God's glory, their joy, and the good of others—men like the one Jesus is forming you to become.

## SEARCHING FOR A MAN

Did you know God is also looking for a man? Ezekiel 22:30 says, "And I sought for a man among them . . ." (KJV).

Second Chronicles 16:9 says, "The eyes of the LORD roam throughout the earth, so that He may strongly support those whose heart is completely His" (NASB).

Tragically, so many men fail to respond to these invitations. But in Jesus you can be the man God is looking for. Because of Jesus' life, death, resurrection, and ascension, you are no longer under Adam who turned away; you are in Christ who embraced the Father's will. He sent his Spirit into your heart to cry "Abba Father." You don't have to slave away in the hope of someday becoming a better man. You don't have to hack your way to health and happiness. You have been given this life and inheritance as a gift.

Jesus went into the heart of the shadows, becoming sin for you. He took on your shame, rejection, isolation, and futility that you could have his grace, power, authority, and kingdom. Jesus' vision of the Father was blocked by the curse of sin, satanic resistance, and human rebellion on the cross. He went to the darkness of the grave that you may live in his light. He was forsaken that you could be accepted, punished that you could be forgiven, cursed that you might inherit his blessing. C. S. Lewis said, "The Son of God became a man to enable men to become sons of God."[9]

You are free from having to try and live up to some idealized Christian standard. You are living out your God-given inheritance and identity in him. That's what Satan is trying to hide. That's what he is trying to stop you from seeing. You are destined to rule and reign as a king and a priest in a new heaven and earth. In fact, creation itself is groaning to be stewarded by the redeemed sons of God. It's waiting for the full work of God in our lives to be revealed.

> Jesus went to the darkness of the grave that you may live in his light.

The J. B. Phillips translation puts it like this: "The whole creation is on tip-toe to see the wonderful sight of the sons of God coming into their own" (Romans 8:18–21). This life is an apprenticeship and training ground for the kingdom to come. So let him transform you into the man you are called to be.

Brother, hear these words from the apostle Paul:

The night is nearly over; the day is almost here. So let us put aside the deeds of darkness and put on the armor of light. Let us behave decently, as in the daytime, not in carousing and drunkenness, not in sexual immorality and debauchery, not in dissension and jealousy. Rather, clothe yourselves with the Lord Jesus Christ, and do not think about how to gratify the desires of the flesh. (Romans 13:12–14)

Face the shadows.
Fight the shadows.
Walk into the light.
We will see you there.

# ACKNOWLEDGMENTS

## JEFFERSON BETHKE

A book is a work of a thousand people in my life directly or indirectly. Below are just a few that I know I couldn't have done this without!

Alyssa and the kids—thank you for allowing me to process this book out loud for years. To work on the ideas. To sharpen them. To hone them. And thank you for the constant help and support. We truly are a team, and I am so thankful for you all.

To Jon—what a wild journey this has been since we met in the basement of Bridgetown Church in Portland. Beyond grateful for you brother!

Curtis and Mike and the entire Yates team—thanks for saying yes to this book idea years ago. We wouldn't be here without you. The way you all have shaped this book, believed in this book, and supported this book humbles me deeply. Thanks for taking a chance on this twenty-two-year-old kid so many years ago!

The Nelson Team (Andrew, Daniel, Chris, John, Lisa, Janene, Emily, and the rest!)—five books and a decade years later, we are still here working together. Y'all are the best in the business, and it shows! Thanks for shepherding our words and carrying so much of this process and getting it from start to finish.

To all the men I look up to—you know who you are. There are dozens of you. You authentically live the life of Jesus and have shown me what it means to be a man in so many areas. Thanks for the brotherhood!

## JON TYSON

I am so grateful for the kind folks who worked to make this book a reality and believed in the need to serve men in our cultural moment.

Jesus, the best man who ever lived. I pray this helps conform more men to your image.

To Christy, for giving me space and encouragement to go after what God has put in my heart.

To my son, Nathan, for helping me become a better father and man.

My daughter, Haley, for reminding me the world needs better men.

To the folks at Church of the City New York for giving me space to run at full speed.

To Jefferson, my coauthor and ministry collaborator. This has been infinitely better doing this with you than on my own.

To Mike and Curtis and the Yates and Yates crew. Thanks for taking a chance on me and reminding me of deadlines:).

To the hardworking folks at Nelson Books:

Andrew Stoddard for saying yes to the book.

Daniel Marrs for your fantastic work with the edits.

John Andrade for spreading the word.

Chris Sigfrids for pushing us forward.

Lisa Beech for giving this book a voice.

# NOTES

## Introduction

1. Henry David Thoreau, *Walden* (London: CRW Publishing, 2004, orig. pub. 1854), 12.
2. Marianne Bertrand and Jessica Pan, "The Trouble with Boys: Social Influences and the Gender Gap in Disruptive Behavior," *American Economic Journal 5*, no. 1 (2013): 32–64, https://doi .org/10.1257/app.5.1.32; Christopher J. Ferguson, "Violent Video Games and Aggression: Causal Relationship or Byproduct of Family Violence and Intrinsic Violence Motivation," *Criminal Justice and Behavior* 35, http://www.asanet.org/wp-content /uploads/soe_july_2016_jayanti_owens_news_release.pdf no. 3 (2008): 311–32, https://doi.org/10.1177/0093854807311719.
3. C. G. Jung, "Psychology and Religion," in *Collected Works of Carl Jung*, volume 11: Psychology and Religion: West and East, 1938, 131.
4. See especially Paul's diagnosis of man's sinful condition in Romans 1:18–32.
5. Robert Bly, *Iron John* (Boston: Da Capo Press, 2015), 43.

## Chapter 1: The Eclipse

1. *300*, directed by Zack Snyder (Burbank: Warner Bros. Studio, 2006).

## Chapter 2: The Shadow of Despair

1. Jed Diamond, "Deaths of Despair: Are Males More Vulnerable?," The Good Men Project, January 21, 2022, https://medium.com /equality-includes-you/deaths-of-despair-are-males-more -vulnerable-f43047d9125d.
2. Diamond, "Deaths of Despair."
3. Brookings Institution, "Addressing America's Crisis of Despair and Economic Recovery: A Call for a Coordinated Effort" (July 2021), https://www.brookings.edu/wp-content/uploads/2021/07 /Addressing-Americas-crisis-despair-economic-recovery.pdf.
4. Christine Emba, "Opinion: Men Are Lost. Here's a Map Out of the Wilderness," *Washington Post*, July 10, 2023, https://www .washingtonpost.com/opinions/2023/07/10/christine-emba -masculinity-new-model/.
5. Ciro Conversano, et al., "Optimism and Its Impact on Mental and Physical Well-Being," *Clinical Practice and Epidemiology in Mental Health* 6 (2010): 25–29, https://www.ncbi.nlm.nih.gov /pmc/articles/PMC2894461/.
6. Viktor Emil Frankl, *Man's Search for Meaning* (Boston: Beacon Press, 2006).
7. Frankl, *Man's Search for Meaning.*
8. Michael Easter, *The Comfort Crisis: Embrace Discomfort to Reclaim Your Wild, Happy, Healthy Self* (Emmaus, PA: Harmony/Rodale, 2021. Kindle Edition), 92.
9. James K. A. Smith, *You Are What You Love: The Spiritual Power of Habit* (Grand Rapids, MI: Brazos Press, 2016), 11.
10. Originally published in N. T. Wright, *The Millennium Myth*, (Louisville, KY: Westminster John Knox Press, 1999), 41.

## Chapter 3: The Shadow of Loneliness

1. Thomas Joiner, *Lonely at the Top: The High Cost of Men's Success* (New York: St. Martin's Press, 2011), 35–36.
2. Joiner, *Lonely at the Top*, 35.

3. Joiner, *Lonely at the Top*, 35.

4. Joiner, *Lonely at the Top*, 36.

5. Joiner, *Lonely at the Top*, 36.

6. Justin Heckert, "The Hazards of Growing Up Painlessly," *New York Times*, November 18, 2012, https://www.nytimes.com /2012/11/18/magazine/ashlyn-blocker-feels-no-pain.html.

7. Julianne Holt-Lunstad, Timothy B. Smith, and J. Bradley Layton, "Social Relationships and Mortality Risk: A Meta-Analytic Review," *PLoS Med* 7, no. 7 (2010), https://doi.org/10.1371 /journal.pmed.1000316.

8. Frank H. Durgin et al., "The Social Psychology of Perception Experiments: Hills, Backpacks, Glucose, and the Problem of Generalizability," *Journal of Experimental Psychology: Human Perception and Performance* 38, no. 6 (2012): 1582–95, https:// www.ncbi.nlm.nih.gov/pmc/articles/PMC3445748/.

9. The Harvard Study and Lifespan Research Foundation website, "Using Research to Promote Human Thriving," Lifespan Research Foundation, https://www.lifespanresearch.org/harvard-study/.

10. Liz Mineo, "Work Out Daily? OK, but How Socially Fit Are You?," *The Harvard Gazette*, February 10, 2023, https://news .harvard.edu/gazette/story/2023/02/work-out-daily-ok-but-how -socially-fit-are-you/.

11. Alex Williams, "Why Is It Hard to Make Friends Over 30?" *New York Times*, July 13, 2012, https://www.nytimes.com/2012/07/15 /fashion/the-challenge-of-making-friends-as-an-adult.html?source =post_page.

12. David Roberts, "How Our Housing Choices Make Adult Friendships More Difficult," Vox, December 27, 2018, https:// www.vox.com/2015/10/28/9622920/housing-adult-friendship.

13. Wendell Berry, "A Native Hill," in *The Art of the Commonplace: The Agrarian Essays of Wendell Berry*, ed. Norman Wirzba (Washington, DC: Counterpoint, 2002), 12.

14. Christopher Dana Lynn, "Hearth and Campfire Influences on Arterial Blood Pressure: Defraying the Costs of the Social Brain Through Fireside Relaxation," *Evolutionary Psychology* 12, no. 5 (November 2014): 983-1003, https://pubmed.ncbi.nlm.nih.gov /25387270/.

15. Eric O. Jacobsen, *Three Pieces of Glass: Why We Feel Lonely in a World Mediated by Screens* (Grand Rapids, MI: Brazos Press, 2020).
16. Michael Easter, *The Comfort Crisis: Embrace Discomfort to Reclaim Your Wild, Happy, Healthy Self* (Emmaus, PA: Rodale Books, 2021).
17. Matthew Woodward, "Netflix Statistics: Is the Platform Still Growing?" Search Logistics, https://www.searchlogistics.com/learn/statistics/netflix-statistics/.
18. "Commuting Crawling Back, Census Bureau Survey Shows," CBS News, September 14, 2023, https://www.cbsnews.com/news/commuting-slow-return-census-bureau-survey/.
19. Laurel Gasque, "Andrei Rublev: The Holy Trinity," ArtWay, https://artway.eu/content.php?id=730&lang=en&action=show.

## Chapter 4: The Shadow of Shame

1. "Shining Light on Shame," Council for Christian Colleges & Universities, panel discussion with Curt Thompson, Angulus Wilson, Steve Beers, and Morgan C. Feddes, Spring 2017, https://CCCU.org/magazine/shining-light-shame/.
2. Curt Thompson, *The Soul of Shame: Retelling the Stories We Believe About Ourselves* (Downers Grove, IL: InterVarsity Press, 2015), 27.
3. C. S. Lewis, *The Great Divorce* (London: HarperCollins, 2012).
4. Robert Bly, *A Little Book on the Human Shadow* (New York: HarperCollins, 1988), 38.
5. Jimmy Stamp, "The Daring Escape from the Eastern State Penitentiary," *Smithsonian Magazine*, November 13, 2013, https://www.smithsonianmag.com/arts-culture/the-daring-escape-from-the-eastern-state-penitentiary-180947688/.

## Chapter 5: The Shadow of Lust

1. Maggie Jones, "What Teenagers Are Learning from Online Porn," *New York Times*, February 7, 2018, https://www.nytimes.com/2018/02/07/magazine/teenagers-learning-online-porn-literacy-sex-education.html?smid=url-share.
2. Emily F. Rothman, Nicole Daley, and Jess Alder, "A Pornography

Literacy Program for Adolescents," *American Journal of Public Health* 110, no. 2 (2020): 154–156, https://ajph.aphapublications.org/doi/full/10.2105/AJPH.2019.305468.

3. Philip Yancey, *A Skeptic's Guide to Faith* (Grand Rapids, MI: Zondervan, 2009), 74.

4. Yancey, *A Skeptic's Guide to Faith*, 80.

5. Yancey, *A Skeptic's Guide to Faith*, 80.

6. Mary Eberstadt, *Adam and Eve After the Pill: Paradoxes of the Sexual Revolution* (San Francisco: Ignatius Press, 2012), 24.

7. Ronald Rolheiser, *The Holy Longing* (New York: Crown Publishing, 2014), 198–199.

8. "How Porn Can Hurt a Consumer's Partner," Fight the New Drug, May 4, 2017, https://fightthenewdrug.org/how-porn-can-hurt-a-consumers-partner/.

9. Vaughan Roberts, *The Porn Problem: Christian Compassion, Convictions and Wisdom for Today's Big Issues* (Epsom, UK: The Good Book Company, 2018), 24.

10. Chuck Klosterman, *Sex, Drugs, and Cocoa Puffs: A Low Culture Manifesto* (New York: Scribner, 2003), 112.

11. Said in a conversation at Praxis Labs Hudson Valley Retreat and Minnewaska Lodge in October 2016.

12. C. S. Lewis, *The Collected Letters of C.S. Lewis, Volume 3*, edited by Walter Hooper (Cambridge: Cambridge University Press, 2007), 158.

13. Ronald Rolheiser, *Wrestling with God* (New York: Crown Publishing, 2018), 61.

14. Bishop of Hippo Saint Augustine, *The Confessions* (New York: Oxford University Press, 2008), 61.

15. G. K. Chesterton, *The Collected Works of G. K. Chesterton,* vol. 1, edited by David Dooley (San Francisco: Ignatius, 1986).

16. Timothy Keller and Kathy Keller, *The Meaning of Marriage* (New York: Penguin Books, 2011), 9.

17. C. S. Lewis, *The Four Loves* (New York: HarperCollins, 2017).

18. "Epistle to Diognetus," trans. by Alexander Roberts and James Donaldson (Moscow, ID: Roman Roads Media, 2015), https://files.romanroadsstatic.com/materials/romans/early-christianity/DiognetusV1-0.pdf.

## Chapter 6: The Shadow of Ambition

1. Donald Whitney, *Simplify Your Spiritual Life: Spiritual Disciplines for the Overwhelmed* (Colorado Springs, CO: NavPress, 2014), Kindle.
2. James K. A. Smith, *On the Road with Saint Augustine* (Grand Rapids, MI: Baker Publishing, 2019), 81.
3. Timothy Dwight, "Sermon XXVII: On the Love of Distinction," in *Sermons*, vol. 1 (Edinburgh: Waugh and Innes, 1828), 512.
4. Smith, *On the Road*, 78.
5. Francis A. Schaeffer, *A Christian Manifesto* (Wheaton, IL: Crossway, 2005), 61.
6. Robert Crosby, "Remembering David Wilkerson," *Christianity Today*, April 29, 2011, https://www.christianitytoday.com/ct /2011/aprilweb-only/rememberingdavidwilkerson.html.
7. A House on Beekman, https://www.ahouseonbeekman.org.
8. Missional Labs website, 2023, https://missionallabs.co/.
9. Jack J. Bauer, Dan P. McAdams, and April R. Sakaeda, "Crystallization of Desire and Crystallization of Discontent in Narratives of Life-Changing Decisions," *Journal of Personality*, 73, no. 5 (2005): 1181–1213, https://doi.org/10.1111/j.1467-6494 .2005.00346.x.
10. "Polycarp's Martyrdom," abridged and modernized by Stephen Tomkins, Christian History Institute, https:// christianhistoryinstitute.org/study/module/polycarp/.
11. *Hotel Rwanda*, directed by Terry George (Beverly Hills, CA: United Artists, 2004).
12. Eugene Peterson, *Working the Angles: The Shape of Pastoral Integrity* (Grand Rapids, MI: Wm. B. Eerdmans, 1987), 44.
13. Jocko Willink and Leif Babin, *Extreme Ownership: How U.S. Navy SEALs Lead and Win* (New York: St. Martin's Press, 2017).

## Chapter 7: The Shadow of Futility

1. Jeanna Smialek, Lydia DePillis, and Ben Castleman, "Why Are Middle-Aged Men Missing from the Labor Market?," *New York*

*Times*, December 2, 2022, https://www.nytimes.com/2022/12/02
/business/economy/job-market-middle-aged-men.html.

2. Andy Crouch, "Flourishing Culture—Andy Crouch," Common
   Good Conference 2017, YouTube video, August 26, 2020, 42:37,
   https://www.youtube.com/watch?v=jQID8QioRcc.

3. The concept of the four levels of ruling was sparked by a
   conversation I (Jeff) had with my mentor and friend Jeremy Pryor,
   with whom I run Family Teams. (You can check out our work at
   www.familyteams.com.).

4. Michael Grunwald, "A Tower of Courage," *Washington Post,*
   October 28, 2001, https://www.washingtonpost.com/archive
   /lifestyle/2001/10/28/a-tower-of-courage/c53e8244-3754-440f
   -84f8-51f841aff6c8/.

5. Grunwald, "A Tower of Courage."

6. N. T. Wright, *After You Believe: Why Christian Character
   Matters* (New York: HarperOne, 2010), 18–22.

7. Stuart Brown, MD, with Christopher Vaughan, *Play: How It
   Shapes the Brain, Opens the Imagination, and Invigorates the
   Soul* (New York: Penguin, 2009), 60.

8. Dr. Stuart Brown, "Play Is More Than Just Fun," Serious Play
   2008, YouTube video, 26:01, May 2008, https://www.ted.com
   /talks/stuart_brown_play_is_more_than_just_fun?language=en.

## Chapter 8: The Shadow of Apathy

1. Check Palahniuk, *Fight Club: A Novel* (New York: W. W. Norton
   and Company, 2018), 166.

2. Derek Thompson, "Colleges Have a Guy Problem," *The Atlantic*,
   September 14, 2021, https://www.theatlantic.com/ideas/archive
   /2021/09/young-men-college-decline-gender-gap-higher-education
   /620066/.

3. This conversation happened at one of our morning men's prayer
   sets at Church of the City New York in September 2021.

4. C. S. Lewis, *The Screwtape Letters* (New York: HarperOne, 2009), 61.

5. Jane McGonigal, "Video Games: An Hour a Day Is Key to
   Success in Life," HuffPost, February 15, 2011, https://www
   .huffpost.com/entry/video-games_b_823208.

6. Roland Hughes, "The Spiderman of Paris: What Happened Next?," BBC News, December 23, 2018, https://www.bbc.com /news/world-europe-46538253.

7. Jeff V. Cook, *Seven: The Deadly Sins and the Beatitudes* (Grand Rapids, MI: Zondervan, 2008), 34.

8. "The Only Thing Necessary for the Triumph of Evil Is for Good Men to Do Nothing," author unknown, Open Culture, March 13, 2016, https://www.openculture.com/2016/03/edmund -burkeon-in-action.html.

9. "General William Booth and the 'I'll Fight' Address," *Caring* magazine, September 5, 2018, https://caringmagazine.org /general-william-booth-and-the-ill-fight-address/.

10. Robert Morris, "STOP Tolerating Jezebel Spirit," 55:30, YouTube video, April 7, 2011, https://www.youtube.com/watch?v= VtW074wfF9o.

## Conclusion and Call

1. James Hollis, *A Life of Meaning* (Louisville, CO: Sounds True, 2023), 51.

2. Hollis, *A Life of Meaning*, 59.

3. Hollis, *A Life of Meaning*, 39.

4. John Steinbeck, *Travels with Charley: In Search of America* (New York: Penguin, 2012), 9.

5. Steinbeck, *Travels with Charley*, 9.

6. Diogenes Laertius et al., *Diogenes of Sinope - Life and Legend: Handbook of Source Material*, 2nd ed., ed. Frank Redmond (Chicago: Mênin Web and Print Publishing, 2016), 74.

7. Joshua J. Mark, "The Life of Diogenes of Sinope in Diogenes Laertius," *World History Encyclopedia*, August 6, 2014, https://www.worldhistory.org/article/740/the-life-of-diogenes -of-sinope-in-diogenes-laertiu/. Diogenes was a true cynic. History recounts "When Plato defined a human being as a 'featherless biped,' Diogenes plucked a chicken and brought it to Plato's Academy. He released it into one of the classrooms, saying, 'Behold – Plato's human being.' Plato was then forced to add 'with broad, flat, nails' to his definition."

8. Some of the bravest men of conviction I know are Side B gay men

living their commitment to Jesus and the historic sexual ethic with fierce loyalty and devotion, though they may not fit into cultural concepts as others define it.

9. C. S. Lewis, *Mere Christianity* (New York: Simon and Schuster, 1996), 155.

# ABOUT THE
# AUTHORS

## JEFFERSON BETHKE

Jefferson Bethke is the *New York Times* bestselling author of *Jesus > Religion* and *Take Back Your Family*. He and his wife, Alyssa, run FamilyTeams.com, an online initiative equipping families to live as a multigenerational team on mission. Jeff serves at formingmen.com with Jon Tyson. Jeff and Alyssa live in Maui with their daughters, Kinsley and Lucy; son, Kannon; and pup, Griffey. To say hi or to learn more, head over to jeffandalyssa.com.

## JON TYSON

Jon Tyson is a pastor and author in New York City. Originally from Adelaide, Australia, Jon moved to the United States two decades ago to seek and cultivate renewal in the Western church. He is the author of the bestselling book *The Intentional Father* and *Beautiful Resistance*. He serves as the lead pastor of Church of the City New York. Jon has been married to Christy for twenty-five years and has two adult children.

# WE'VE GOT A
# FREE GIFT
# FOR YOU

## TO THANK YOU FOR
## FINISHING THE BOOK!

SCAN THE CODE BELOW TO
CLAIM IT AT FORMINGMEN.COM

**FORMING
MEN**

# ANOTHER BONUS:

# JON'S WEEKLY NEWSLETTER

EVERY WEEK JON SENDS OUT A 500-800 WORD ESSAY FOR MEN AND FATHERS.

SCAN BELOW TO START GETTING IT SENT STRAIGHT TO YOUR INBOX.

**FORMING MEN**